Poetry as Prayer
Gerard Manley Hopkins

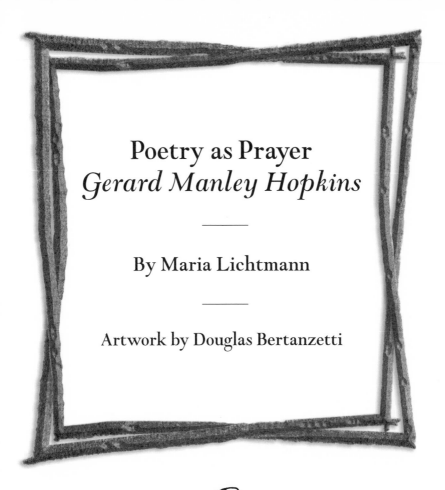

Poetry as Prayer
Gerard Manley Hopkins

———

By Maria Lichtmann

———

Artwork by Douglas Bertanzetti

Pauline
BOOKS & MEDIA
BOSTON

Library of Congress Cataloging-in-Publication Data

Lichtmann, Maria R., 1945–

  Poetry as prayer : Gerard Manley Hopkins / by Maria Lichtmann ; artwork by Douglas Bertanzetti.

    p. cm. — (The poetry as prayer series)

Includes bibliographical references.

  ISBN 0-8198-5936-2

  1. Hopkins, Gerard Manley, 1844–1889—Criticism and interpretation. 2. Christian poetry, English—History and criticism. 3. Hopkins, Gerard Manley, 1844–1889—Religion. 4. Sonnets, English—History and criticism. 5. Prayer in literature. I. Title. II. Series.

  PR4803.H44 Z71165 2002

                     2002002679

The Scripture quotations contained herein are from the *New Revised Standard Version Bible. Catholic Edition,* copyright © 1993 and 1989 by the Division of Christian Education of the National Council of Churches of Christ in the U.S.A. Used by permission. All rights reserved.

Cover design by Helen Rita Lane, FSP

Printed and published in the U.S.A. by Pauline Books & Media, 50 Saint Pauls Avenue, Boston, MA 02130-3491.

www.pauline.org

Pauline Books & Media is the publishing house of the Daughters of St. Paul, an international congregation of women religious serving the Church with the communications media.

1 2 3 4 5 6   07 06 05 04 03 02

Dedicated to my husband,
Robert Schneider

Contents

Foreword

Telling of the hungers of the human heart, the contemporary poet David Whyte writes: "One good word is bread for a thousand." Each of the words of Gerard Manley Hopkins is like a warm, crusty, hearty loaf that has fed thousands over the years and across the miles. His is a thick, dense creation, a language *of* contemplation and a language *for* contemplation, inviting us to recognize that "Christ plays in ten thousand places."

Contemplation is, above all, a way of seeing: the more we see, the more we love; the more we love, the more we see. Love has a look. Hopkins was a looker, one who could see into the *thing-ness,* or *is-ness,* of things. He was an astute observer of nature and a lover of language. He knew that the contemplative task is one of seeing and saying: learning how to see and then saying what we see.

The wisdom of the ages holds that we find ourselves, and God, by the long journey inward, by a deeper and deeper penetration of the deepest recesses of the soul or, in today's terms, the self. Hopkins moved precisely in the opposite direction. His quest for God was outbound, looking upon and into everything and everyone, beholding the presence of God in brokenness and in beauty, in regions of woundedness as well as of wisdom.

Hopkins sees into things. When we linger long and lovingly with Hopkins we look with love, and see the love loose in the world. Everything then shimmers with life, and we are one with it all. With God. In the simple act of looking. Of beholding.

Maria Lichtmann's words are themselves an exercise in contemplative prayer, inviting the reader to see the luminous link between art and theology, the holy and the beautiful. Her reading of Hopkins is singularly fresh and original. Only a deeply contemplative eye such as Lichtmann's can read Hopkins with such clarity: as priest and poet whose most priestly act was his poetry; as one who was marginal even in his own religious community; as a soul "doomed to succeed by failure." Above all, he was one gifted with the graced affliction of seeing and saying in a way that others could not appreciate or comprehend during his own lifetime. But his words continue to give life and strength beyond his own time and place.

Lichtmann invites us to pause, to ponder, to gaze, to behold Hopkins' words, to allow ourselves to be carried by them, buoyed up by them. She bids us to pray with Hopkins, gently guiding us to receive the gift of contemplation through the act of quiet, holy reading. As an expert teacher and spiritual guide, she leads us in the ancient discipline of *lectio divina,* described by the early desert fathers and mothers as a way of chewing and savoring, indeed swallowing, each word of a sacred text.

Open the pages of Maria Lichtmann's volume as you would lift, bless, and break a warm and crusty bread. Then chew and savor the mix of good words in Hopkins and in Lichtmann, a braided loaf to feed a thousand.

Michael Downey
Professor of Systematic Theology and Spirituality
Saint John's Seminary, Camarillo

Chapter 1

Poetry as Prayer

Poetry and the Sacred

Poetry was once the language of the sacred. In all the sacred scriptures of the world, poetry rather than prose expressed the sacred character of existence. Where other words failed, poetry's "hints and guesses,"[1] its sparseness of words, special rhythms, and use of metaphor, came closest expressing the inexpressible. The oldest sacred stories and words of a people, including the oldest language of the Bible, were originally poetic in form. Even the oracles of the prophets were filled with the parallelism and rhythm of Hebrew poetry. When ancient peoples chose to pray, their speech and song became poetic.

For that reason, poetry can bind us back to the sacred; it can lead us to prayer in its earliest, most sacred form. Its very repetitions of sound and meaning—its turning back on itself—is a religious act, for *re-ligio* means "to bind back" or "to link again." Our way to recover language's sacred character today is through poetry. Because it belongs to the infancy of every people, learning to appreciate poetry means becoming a child again, listening for language at play, and wondering at life's mystery.

It is difficult to imagine living a spiritual life, a life of hearkening to the Spirit, without some form of poetry. In times of personal or communal tragedy, its ability to renew the human spirit and heal hearts broken with grief gives it an unrivaled spiritual power. Without poetry, the soul cannot sing. Even the prose works of mystics like St. John of the Cross and St. Francis of Assisi approach poetry in their lyrical descriptions of union with God. In the liturgy, our communal experience of prayer, we leave our ordinary duties behind to enter liturgical time, the *in illo tempore*, the time that never was yet always is. We take the ordinary things of our lives: words, actions, objects—like bread and wine—and "sacralize" them; each becomes *liminal*. There, on the borders of time and eternity, they suggest to us that everything and all time is holy. Liturgical language reflects that heightened engagement with the ordinary by its elevation toward the poetic. So, in a way, when we read a poem, we enter that liminal experience of time out of time, what some have called *kairos*, where we lose track of time.

Reading Poetry as Prayer

Though poetry has connections to the sacred not only in the past but here and now, in our age, imbued with secular assumptions about literature and art, we may no longer hear its prayerful whispers. We may need to relearn the art of reading poetry as prayer. Reading poetry invites prayer through a process the early monastics called *lectio divina* or "sacred reading." Those who practice the *lectio divina* of the Scriptures begin with reading, move on to meditation or reflection, go deeper into the heart's prayer, and ultimately are invited to contemplative union with God. Carthusian monks call this gradual deepening of *lectio divina* the "journey of the heart." If we are willing, great poetry enables us to make this journey. The following lines from a poem by William Carlos Williams testify to our need for poetry and our tendency to avoid it out of an insatiable desire for "news":

> Look at
>   what passes for the new.
> You will not find it there but in
>   despised poems.
> It is difficult
> to get the news from poems

yet men die miserably every day
for lack of what is found there.[2]

The esteemed monk and scholar of monasticism, Dom Jean LeClerq, once said that when we celebrate the gift of existence, we are praying. "I pray, therefore I exist." Whenever we proclaim our existence and accept ourselves in the presence of ultimate mystery *that* is prayer. This proclamation of existence and of our presence here is the simple task of poetry. Gerard Manley Hopkins said, "nothing is so pregnant and straightforward to the truth as simple *yes* and *is*."[3] In poetry, whether explicitly religious or not, we engage in the great "yes" to our existence and an openness to the mystery of it all. Hopkins understood this "yes" and it entered into all of his poetry, even his most painful sonnets. He knew that his poetry's purpose was to bear witness to all of existence. In a letter to his friend and former tutor, Canon Richard Watson Dixon, he wrote, "all the world is full of things that go unwitnessed..." In one poem, he wrote, "With witness I speak this." His poetic witness constitutes an affirmation of the world in its beauty and its pain. It is the particular stamp of his poetry to witness to the beauty and goodness of creation as well as to the poignancy of human life.

5

Poetry and Silence

Today we are overloaded with more words than ever before in the history of humankind. Unless we live in a cave or hermitage, 24-hour cable news, print, and virtual print literally bombard us in greater quantities and in more media than ever. As the number of words and the ways to reach us expand exponentially, words become cheaper and more profane (no longer sacred) all the time. Our ability to hear them as meaningful diminishes. We live in what the Georgetown University linguist, Deborah Tannen, has called an "argument culture." Although honest and probing discourse still exists, for the most part contentious words bark at us over the airwaves. Some commentators, playwrights, and other wordsmiths increase expletives and turn up the volume in an attempt to regain some of the same power words once had. Words have lost not only their sacredness, but also their depth and richness of meaning; words like "love" and "truth" have become trivialized and overused. Thomas Merton once commented that saying "God is love" today means as much as "eat your Wheaties." As poets themselves have reminded us, though we are drowning in verbiage, yet we are thirsting in a drought of holy words.

Poetry in some form saves us from drowning. Poetry washes us up on an island where the very economy of language makes each word count. The poet Kathleen Norris spoke to a gathering of laypeople and the monks of Gethsemani, saying, "being a poet is keeping words alive and sacred apart from our use of them." Poetry's silences are eloquent. The poet does not ramble, but points. In her poem titled "Ascension," Kathleen Norris points to "the lilac in bud by my front door / bent low / by last week's ice storm" to speak of the Ascension of Christ as well as her sister's experience of childbirth.[4]

Like prayer, poetry participates in the mystery of the relation between speech and silence; indeed, poetry speaks the language of silence. The words of poetry are embraced by silence as the white space that surrounds the printed poem embraces it in the greater space of infinity. Poetry stands at the gateway to a silence that is pregnant with more meaning than most of our words convey. Poetry's *liminal* language stands on the threshold of mystery and of hope; perhaps because a poem dances on the edge of mystery, it moves us in the direction of hope. Poetry leaps from the silence of mystery, the silence of contemplation, as the *Book of Wisdom* says: "When peaceful silence lay over all, and night had run the half of her swift course, down from the heavens, from the royal throne, leapt your all-powerful Word..." (18:14). Poetry gives birth to the word through silence.

Because it keeps faith with silence, poetic language must convey both more and less than prose. The poet, Patricia Hampl, has said, "prose is a job, but poetry is a visitation."[5] Its "more" has to do with intensity, emotion, a heightened personal experience that often speaks in the "I-Thou" language of prayer and relationship. In poetry, the personal voice makes its shy appearance in a culture where impersonal exchanges tend to dominate everyday life. Poetry's "less" involves fewer details than the prosaic accounts of an experience. Poetry clears a space for us where in some way we can turn down the high volume of constant noise, listen to the silence, and move away from the clutter. In a culture of excess, poetry offers us balance.

Along with wordiness, our culture may be characterized by its literal-mindedness, scientific and journalistic language becoming the norm for all language. Rarely in the public square does language take us to our hearts, its metaphors come alive, its images take flight. Much of our daily conversation trades abstractions like so many tokens,

"My winter world, that scarcely breathes that bliss..."

scarcely ever stopping to cash them in for reality. After a couple years of graduate school, I found myself awash in factotums of information, in journalese, academic and business jargons, barely ever getting at their meanings. During a weekend I spent with a contemplative community chanting the Liturgy of the Hours, I was enabled to enter a world saturated with meaning. I began to realize that, although I had acquired much knowledge, I had not allowed it to affect my life and my inmost thinking.

In liturgy, that is, in the praying of the psalms of the Liturgy of the Hours and at the celebration of the Eucharist, we engage in events of great metaphorical power. Along with poetry, Liturgy is one of the few places that continue to nourish our imaginations. The metaphoric language of poetry, where one thing relates to another, suggests the interconnectedness of all experience. While metaphors, symbols, and images become dead as doornails in daily speech, in poetry—as in liturgy—they are still alive, still opening up the hidden riches of reality.

The Poem as Sacrament

Poems entrust their deepest meanings and aspirations to the material level of sound and image and metaphor. These sounds and images and metaphors *embody* the spirit.

In that sense, the poem functions as a sacrament, an outer sign of inner grace. In all poetry, there is a tendency to unify the objective and subjective worlds. For Hopkins, perhaps more than most poets, the outward beauty of the world could be experienced as a sacrament of its inward beauty and grace. He wanted to communicate that sacramental experience through his poems. Hopkins found Christ woven into the fabric of the external realities of nature as their inner design,[6] and he has communicated Christ's real presence in his poems. Each poem is a sacrament of the encounter with Christ, not only in the sense of embodying spirit in matter, but in its ability to change the reader. For Hopkins, poetry conveys the real presence of Christ as does the Eucharist. Further, it conveys Christ's transforming stress, the stress of the Holy Spirit which makes possible the reader's own transformation. It is not too much to say that in his life and poetry, Hopkins is himself a sacrament of the encounter with God.

My own experience with Hopkins' poetry has changed with each new reading. During my freshman and sophomore years of college, a French professor gave me the pocket Penguin edition of Hopkins' poetry, which I carried around as a treasure, though I did not understand it at all. Later, the poem, "Spring and Fall," surprised me with its honesty. It subverted the usual pious common-places about suffering and death and confronted the very real sense of loss and mortality that we all face deep down. From that point on, I was alert to a new dimension in reading this poet. My later discovery of Hopkins' "terrible sonnets," called such because they are so filled with darkness and terror, confirmed my sense that this poet, like the psalmists before, had dared to enter rather than deflect his inner pain. But it was only while I was a postulant in a contemplative religious order that I first began to truly drink in the poetry of Gerard Manley Hopkins like new wine. Somehow, in a contemplative setting, amid the regular recitation of the psalms during the Liturgy of the Hours, his poetry began to speak to me in new ways. I remember creeping down to the convent library during the nightly Grand Silence to memorize whole sections of "The Wreck of the Deutschland." I felt my spirit nourished by the power and beauty of his words. I did not know it then, but I was reading Hopkins in that slow, meditative reading of a *lectio divina* that feeds the soul.

Hopkins' Integrity

During graduate school, my appreciation of Hopkins' poetry deepened immensely. Although Hopkins experienced a wrenching conflict between his priestly and poetic vocations, I found in his poems, letters, and spiritual writings, a profound integrity. I discovered that this poet's life and poetry—in its agonies and its ecstasies—were all of a piece. His aesthetic, spiritual, and personal dimensions were disparate threads woven into an intricate fabric of lights and darks. Encountering this integrity had a profound effect on me. I saw in this man's public and private expressions an utter sincerity and honesty that challenged me to "go and do likewise," especially in regard to my academic work on him and his poetry.

Hopkins' integrity is even more remarkable when we consider that, with one or two exceptions, no one understood or appreciated his poems. His best friend and fellow poet, Robert Bridges, continually charged him with obscurity. In his 1918 publication of Hopkins' sonnets, Bridges' accused them of "blemishes" and "extravagances." Yet, despite the absence of any critical or popular acclaim, Hopkins had the integrity and the courage to be faithful to his own particular gift, his "inscape." Today, at last, Hopkins has found an audience that appreciates both his stylistic experiments and the deeply religious insights they serve to highlight.

Reading Hopkins' Poetry as Prayer

Hopkins' poetry is an incarnational one that can be appreciated only if matter and spirit, form and content, come together in an inseparable unity. Hopkins himself said in writing about poetry: "thought and expression [are] indistinguishable."[7] If we can grapple with both the form and the content, we will have an incarnational experience of the poems. Written with such deep feelings of exuberance or of desperation, they reach to the depths of the self, but they *enact* that feeling in their very form. Several times, Hopkins offered a contemplative hermeneutic of reading or, because he preferred them to be read aloud, hearing his poems. The abiding energy of contemplation is the response appropriate to the inscape, the pattern or design carrying the inner meaning, of Hopkins' verse. Defending the lack of clarity in his poetry to Bridges, Hopkins suggested that he "read it so that lines and stanzas should be left in the memory and superficial impressions deepened.... I am sure I have read and enjoyed pages of poetry that way."[8]

More than most, lines of Hopkins' poems seem to abide, to take root in the memory and then in the heart where they re-emerge in moments of joy or of despair. People have told me that they remember such lines as

"Let him easter in us, be a dayspring to the dimness of us, be a crimson-cresseted east," and in remembering—even if unintentionally—they are praying, because the line itself is a prayer. The poems lead naturally into *lectio divina* with its four-fold process. To read Hopkins' poetry as prayer is to read with the whole self: senses, mind, heart, and soul—and to be challenged to undergo transformation.[9]

Every poem is like a letter sent from the poet to the reader. To read and understand the sender and his "letters" fully, it is necessary to know something of this poet's life, of the life experiences that shaped the man and his poetry.

CHAPTER 2

Gerard Manley Hopkins: A Life

Early Years

In one sense, Hopkins' life was not very remarkable. He had an ordinary upbringing in an ordinary English family, which belonged to the Church of England. Born July 28, 1844, in the village of Stratford outside London, Gerard Manley Hopkins was the first of Manley and Kate Hopkins' nine children. When the family had grown to five children, they moved to Hampstead, a fashionable suburb just north of London. Hopkins' mother, Kate, was interested in music and poetry as well as philosophy and political discussion. Among Kate's siblings there were painters and musicians. Manley Hopkins was an insurance adjustor for shipwrecks, but also wrote poetry, some of which was published. When Hopkins was ten, he was enrolled in Highgate School, a private school just across the Heath from their house on Oak Hill. Hopkins came to dislike this school, and with good reason. The headmaster, a Reverend John Bradley Dyne, had a penchant for beating the boys with his riding whip. The young

Hopkins, though a model student, had a slightly rebellious streak, which emerged more than once in a minor infraction of the rules, such as not going to bed after "Lights Out."[1] For this infringement, the headmaster demoted him to the lowest rank of prefects and refused to recommend him for a scholarship.

Aspects of Hopkins' character were formed at Highgate. Despite his difficulties, Gerard distinguished himself there, winning prizes for poetry, Latin, classics, and, finally, even without the headmaster's recommendation, winning an "Exhibition" (scholarship) to attend Oxford University. His classmates remember him as "full of *fun*, rippling over with jokes and chaff, facile with pencil and pen, with rhyming jibe or cartoon."[2] This fun-loving, mischievous side of his nature never left him, and, in later life, some spoke of it as his "eccentricity."

Hopkins' younger brother, Cyril, remembered another side of his character: his self-denial. As a student at Highgate, after hearing stories of the deprivation suffered by sailors while out at sea, Hopkins gave up all liquids for a week out of sympathy. Cyril later called his brother's tendency to self-denial "moral courage." This predilection to asceticism was to surface several times in Hopkins' early years.

Hopkins was remarkably small in stature and, somewhat frail, did not participate in sports. But he loved to climb to the top of tall trees and enjoy the view. He grew up surrounded by the countryside of Hampstead, now a suburb of London, but then a heath of gorse and broom bushes where sheep grazed and where one could see the city from its highest point. Hopkins would often take the path, edged by hedgerows and oak trees, through Oak Hill Fields on his way to school. Even as a boy natural beauty held a fascination for him.

He began to write poetry at an early age. When he was fifteen, his poem, "The Escorial," won him the poetry prize at Highgate. This ambitious fifteen-stanza poem celebrates in detail the heroic martyrdom of St. Laurence as well as the Blessed Virgin playing tenderly with her child. The poem may be a hint of Hopkins' early religious ideals since it introduces the aspirations, which eventually led to his becoming a Roman Catholic and entering the Society of Jesus (a religious order dedicated to heroic ideals and service, with its share of martyrs). Two years later, he won another school prize with a richly sensuous poem, "A Vision of the Mermaids." Even in these early poems, his own distinctive style and genius as a poet began to shine: "Plum-purple was the west; but spikes of light / Speared open lustrous gashes, crimson-white." Hopkins was already absorbing and even surpassing the styles of such great romantic poets as Byron and Keats. This level of achievement for such a young man was extraordinary. Later, when he looked back on this period of his life, he described himself as a "very conceited boy."[3]

The conflicting ideals of heroic self-sacrifice and ascetic self-denial in his behavior and sensuous abundance and excess in his poetry remained two poles of Hopkins' complex nature throughout his life. Both of these made him the great poet he is. Without asceticism to temper his love of sensory beauty, his life and poetry would have become excessive and cloying. Without his intense love of beauty, in all its particular, minute manifestations, his poetry would have been sterile. Nevertheless, these two tendencies made for an uneasy mixture. One eventually found realization in Hopkins' vocation as a priest, the other in his vocation as a poet. However, one could argue that his most priestly act was the creation of his poetry.

Oxford

After Highgate School, with its strict rules enforced by a harsh headmaster, Hopkins embarked on the freest, happiest period of his life. When he went to Oxford in the spring of 1863, an intellectual, artistic, and religious world of immense significance opened up to him. With his own gifts and temperament, Hopkins was especially well suited to avail himself of all that Oxford had to offer. In letters home to his family, he wrote, "everything is delightful." He made new friends quickly, and with an enthusiasm for each individual. He was often invited to "wines" and breakfasts where he met and conversed with fellow undergraduates. The new student, taking up rooms at the top of a staircase in Balliol College, said, "I have the best views in Balliol."[4] He wrote home that he was "almost too happy," perhaps feeling a bit apologetic for being so happy away from home.

The Oxford of 1863 was a charmingly beautiful place, as Hopkins describes in his poem, "Duns Scotus's Oxford": a "towery city" with trees "branchy between towers;/ Cuckoo-echoing, bell-swarmèd, lark-charmèd...river-rounded." Walking back through Port Meadows along the Cherwell River, Hopkins rejoiced at the view of Oxford's dreamy spires.

Balliol College, one of the premier residential colleges at Oxford, was extremely well regarded for its curriculum in "Greats," a course of study which today might be called the humanities. Balliol, already known for its exceptional professors, also gained a reputation during this period for its "Broad Church" or liberal thinking in regard to theology and Scripture. No one exemplified this thinking more than Benjamin Jowett, a superb classicist and an excellent translator of Plato. Undergraduates worked somewhat independently, but wrote papers for their tutors each week. As Hopkins' primary tutor, Jowett introduced his new pupil to Plato, guided his choice of classes, his prayer in daily chapel, and even his money management. His Broad Church views, however, seemed to have little effect on Hopkins, whose undergraduate essays reveal a strong interest in the philosophy of Plato, but little interest in Jowett's historical-critical discussion of the Bible.

Though Jowett was Hopkins' tutor for a long time, three other outstanding men of Oxford, John Ruskin, Walter Pater, and John Henry Newman, had a greater influence on him when it came to the most important decision of his life. Though no longer at Oxford, Ruskin influenced Hopkins through his books on painting that taught him to "look severely at things apart from their associations," as Hopkins put it in an undergraduate essay.[5] This "innocence of eye," which Hopkins himself later called "chastity of mind," became one of his greatest gifts as a poet, a gift he conveyed to his readers. Ruskin's search for the "ideal form" in nature may have influenced Hopkins' idea of *inscape*. But even more significant for Hopkins' later development was Ruskin's belief that the beauty of art reflected and participated in divine beauty. Ruskin taught Hopkins that it was possible to join art with theology, the holy with the beautiful.

Another of Hopkins' great mentors at Oxford was Walter Pater, Jowett's protégé. Pater coached Hopkins for his final examinations. While Pater believed in the moral value of art, he considered himself an atheist, and Hopkins once recalled having listened to Pater speaking for "two hours against Christianity."[6] Hopkins did not hold Pater's atheism against him, and even continued his friendship when he returned to Oxford as a Jesuit priest. However, Hopkins' ability to accept people where they were was sometimes at odds with his desire for their conversion, as he once admitted bluntly to Bridges.

All his life Hopkins seemed to relish entertaining the opposites that existed within him, and his poetry offers plentiful evidence that faith and doubt coexisted in him. At about the same time that he wrote his early poem, "The Habit of Perfection," expressing a desire to immerse himself in the "elected silence" of a religious life, he also wrote, "Nondum," where he prays to a silent God ("And Thou art silent, whilst Thy world / Contends about its many creeds") to dispel his doubts and speak to his heart. The agonies of religious doubt would return in the "terrible sonnets," written at a period of more excruciating spiritual pain toward the end of his life. These poems of anguished prayer, composed "in extremity," form a frame around Hopkins' poetry of sheer exuberance and praise— a different kind of prayer—during his middle years.

The opposing poles of faith and doubt seemed embodied in two of his great guides—Pater on the one hand and John Henry Newman on the other. It was as if the opposites Hopkins recognized in himself and expressed in his poems also lived in his choice of mentors. The aesthete Pater was as different from John Henry Newman as could be imagined. But it was Newman whose influence penetrated Hopkins' mind and heart most deeply and endured the longest. Like Ruskin, Newman no longer taught at Oxford, and yet, as one of the founders of the Oxford Movement—the great movement of renewal within the Church of England (which can be compared to the twentieth century's Second Vatican Council)— Newman remained a towering spiritual presence. As someone who had made the wrenching decision to leave the Anglican Church and who had paid an enormous price for his conversion to Catholicism, Newman was the model on whom Hopkins relied in his struggle toward Catholicism. In the summer of 1866, Hopkins turned to Newman when he realized the "impossibility of staying in the Church of England."[7] We might well ask why Hopkins made this choice? Two years earlier, Hopkins had written to a friend from Highgate School, giving an account of the motives for his decision:

> The great aid to belief and object of belief is the doctrine of the Real Presence in the Blessed Sacrament of the Altar. Religion without that is sombre, dangerous, illogical, with that it is—not to speak of its grand consistency and certainty—*loveable*. Hold that and you will gain all Catholic truth.[8]

It was belief in the Real Presence that led him into the Catholic Church and shaped the rest of his intellectual, spiritual, and emotional life. Despite his family's insistence that he wait until graduation to enter the Church, Hopkins wrote to Newman saying he was "anxious to become a Catholic." Newman responded, as he always did, with wisdom and temperance, counseling him "to be led on by the Grace of God step by step" and to stay at

Oxford to finish his degree. Finally, Hopkins passionately explained to Newman:

> I now see the alternative thrown open, either to live without Church and sacraments or else, in order to avoid the Catholic Church, to have to attend constantly the services of that very Church. This brings the matter to an absurdity and makes me think that any delay, whatever relief it may be to my parents, is impossible. I am asking you then whether I shall at all costs be received at once.

Newman replied: "you have my best prayers that He who has begun the good work in you may finish it—and I do not doubt He will."

Another person who had a profound effect on Hopkins—and presumably on his decision to become Catholic—was Digby Dolben, a young Protestant man who developed a passionate interest in things medieval and Catholic, even to the point of donning a monastic habit. Dolben passed through Hopkins' life very briefly on a visit to Oxford, but Dolben's untimely death by drowning only added pathos to Hopkins' life-long memory of the man. During his undergraduate years, Hopkins began keeping a list of his sins for confession, and among these notes is found the sonnet, "Where art thou friend?" which expresses sorrow over Dolben's departure from Oxford. At Dolben's death, Hopkins wrote to Bridges, "I looked forward to meeting Dolben and his being a Catholic more than to anything."[9]

A New Life

In this age of ecumenism and tolerance, we cannot fully understand the terrible consequences Hopkins was prepared to accept because of his decision to convert to Catholicism. First, it caused an estrangement from his parents that he felt throughout his life. So disconnected was his family from him in this most precious decision of his life, twenty years later, he wrote in "To seem the stranger" (*Poems* 66) that his "Father and mother dear, / Brothers and sisters [were] in Christ not near." He also lost ground in his relationship with the leaders of the Oxford Movement, Reverend Henry Parry Liddon and Reverend Edward Pusey, his confessor and spiritual advisor. Liddon wrote four letters imploring Hopkins to change his mind, and in one of these told him that his father had written him in "deep sorrow." Despite these entreaties, before his graduation from Oxford in 1866, Hopkins presented himself to Newman at his Birmingham Oratory to be received into the Catholic Church.

In addition to the painful renunciations already mentioned, there may well have been a more hidden one. Hopkins received the highest honors upon his graduation from Oxford. We can speculate that if not for his decision to leave the Anglican Church, he might well have been offered a career as Fellow of an Oxford college. In choosing to become a Catholic, Hopkins gave up any security with regard to his family, friends, and the choice of his life's work.

Real Presence

Belief in the Real Presence of Christ in the sacrament of the Eucharist was to be the touchstone of Hopkins' entire religious life, and indeed, of his entire life (for the two were inseparable). Hopkins *loved* Christ in the Eucharist in a way he never loved before. This awakening of love through belief in the Real Presence led directly to the central role the Incarnation played in his life. In a letter, Hopkins declared that "the trivialness of life is...done away by the Incarnation."[10] At the end of his life, he said, "My life is determined by the Incarnation down to the smallest details of the day."[11] (We will explore this dominant theme further in the next chapter.)

Besides his decision to convert to Catholicism, another choice remained for Hopkins, and it proved just as difficult and life defining as the first. Following Hopkins' conversion and graduation, Newman offered the new convert a position as tutor in the boys' school he had set up at the Oratory in Birmingham. Hopkins agreed despite his own distaste for early schooling because of his experience at Highgate and his feeling that teaching was "burdensome, especially when you have much of it."[12] He stayed only about half a year, because at an Easter retreat, he decided to become a Jesuit. He wrote about his decision to a friend who had been with him at Oxford:

> I am expecting to take orders and soon, but I wish it to be secret till it comes about. Besides that it is the happiest and best way it practically is the only one. You know I once wanted to be a painter. But even if I could I wd. not I think, now, for the fact is that the higher and more attractive parts of the art put a strain upon the passions which I shd. think it unsafe to encounter. I want to write still and as a priest I very likely can do that too, not so freely as I shd. have liked, e.g. nothing or little in the verse way, but no doubt what wd. best serve the cause of my religion. But if I am a priest it will cause my mother, or she says it will, great grief and this preys on my mind very much and makes the near prospect quite black. The general result is that I am perfectly

reckless about things that I shd. otherwise care about...and this state of mind, though it is painful coming to, when reached gives a great and real sense of freedom.[13]

Hopkins, who had been unsure which order to enter, being "doubtful between St. Benedict and St. Ignatius," shared his decision to join the Jesuits with his esteemed adviser, Newman, who responded with these important words:

> I am both surprised and glad at your news.... I think it is the very thing for you.... The Benedictines would not have suited you. Do not call the Jesuit discipline hard; it will bring you to heaven.
>
> We all congratulate you.
> Ever yours affectionately,
> John H. Newman[14]

In characteristic fashion, Hopkins went beyond what would have been expected of him. During a retreat with the Jesuits at Manresa House (named for the place where St. Ignatius began to compose his *Spiritual Exercises* in 1522), at Roehampton, then a village over five miles from London, he decided to burn all of his poems. In his journal entry for May 11, 1868, Hopkins recorded this cryptic phrase, "Slaughter of the innocents," which almost certainly refers to his earlier resolution to "give up all beauty until he had / His leave [that is, permission] for it."[15] Judging from the letter quoted above, Hopkins must have felt that his Jesuit vocation would leave no room for such an "indulgence" as poetry. Father Christopher Devlin, editor of Hopkins' sermons and spiritual writings, comments, "His poetic genius was his very essence, his 'inscape,' his special likeness to the Divine Essence. Yet Hopkins the Jesuit behaved to Hopkins the poet as a Victorian husband might to a wife of whom he had cause to be ashamed."[16]

Jesuit Spirituality

In choosing the Jesuits rather than the Benedictines, Hopkins made yet another difficult choice. Throughout the nineteenth century, the Jesuits were out of favor in England to the extent that they had actually been outlawed. Perhaps it was this forbidden status of the Jesuit community that drew Hopkins to them. As a Catholic and then a Jesuit, Hopkins had chosen to become doubly the outsider. Further, within this community of individuals who trained to go to the missions alone, Hopkins' life became one of increasing isolation and loneliness. From

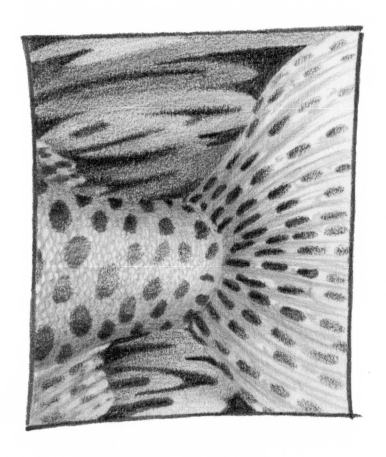

"Glory be to God for dappled things—"

the beginning, the life was hard, as Hopkins predicted to Newman it would be. As new recruits, these "soldiers of Christ" who followed St. Ignatius, rose at 5:30 from their dormitory cubicles, meditated for an hour, celebrated the Eucharist, ate a breakfast of porridge at 7:45, received instructions on the rule, and began the day's manual labor inside (sweeping and cleaning bathrooms), and outside (tending the gardens and livestock, or digging). Then it was back to chapel for prayer—all before dinner at 1 P.M.!

Shortly after Hopkins' arrival on September 18, 1868, he made the "Long Retreat" of thirty days using the *Spiritual Exercises* of St. Ignatius, the first of many he would make during his twenty years as a Jesuit. The four "weeks" of the *Exercises* involve intense meditation on the life of Christ, as well as on the two standards: "the one of Christ our supreme Captain and Lord; the other of Lucifer, the mortal enemy of our human nature," and on the choice to be made between them.[17] To make Christ the standard of one's life means a life of poverty and reproach. Perhaps the *Exercises* offer a glimpse into the reason why Hopkins chose the life of hardship with the Jesuits over any other. All his life Hopkins had felt attracted to heroism, and becoming a Catholic was a heroic choice. In becoming a Jesuit, he opted for the heroic ideal, which

Ignatius had presented to the men of his Order: to fight under the standard of Christ, refusing riches and honor. Perhaps Hopkins saw in the rigorous lifestyle of the novitiate and Jesuit life a chance to practice the asceticism that had attracted him as a schoolboy.

However, heroic self-sacrifice was not Hopkins' sole or chief attraction to Jesuit spirituality. In addition to the Ignatian emphasis on the *via negativa*, was the positive way, the *via positiva* of finding God in all created things. In the *Exercises* Ignatius wrote that God is to be found "in the elements, giving them being; in the plants, giving them life; in the animals, giving them sensation; in human beings, giving them understanding."[18] In this sense, Jesuit spirituality confirmed Hopkins' already great inclination, which had been refined through his reading of Ruskin, to see the world as it really is: good, and even more, holy.

Priest and Poet

After his novitiate, Hopkins was sent to St. Beuno's in Wales for the study of theology, the next step in his Jesuit formation. St. Beuno's College, a massive gray building crowned with an assortment of gables and towers, stood on the hillside of "Moel Maenefa" commanding a spectacular view of the Valley of the Clywd. The lush, green valley opened wide for miles in all directions stretching toward the sea to the north and the mountains of Snowdon to the south. Gardens behind the college climbed "seemingly up to heaven" as Hopkins put it. Delighted with the landscape of his new home, he wrote lyrically in his journal, "All the length of the valley, the skyline of hills was flowingly written all along upon the sky.... I felt an instress and charm of Wales."[19] In this vast, open valley, Hopkins' poetic impulse, which had been suppressed and dormant, now opened up once more. The enjoyment he had always taken in the "inscape" and "instress"—his own coined words—of the natural world, sometimes confided to his journals, again found expression in poetry.

But since the burning of his early poems and his entrance into the Jesuit order seven years earlier, Hopkins had imposed silence on his poetic self. He felt that his vocation to the priesthood demanded total loyalty, which ruled out any other vocation. He desired to be completely faithful to Christ, even if it cost him dearly. Only as an act of obedience would he allow himself to take up his poetic vocation anew. Hopkins' poetic powers were reawakened thanks to a random remark of his superior.

In a letter to a fellow poet and former teacher, Dixon, Hopkins explained how this conjunction of perfect obedience and newfound freedom to write poetry came about:

> [W]hen in the winter of '75 the Deutschland was wrecked in the mouth of the Thames and five Franciscan nuns, exiles from Germany by the Falck Laws, aboard of her were drowned, I was affected by the account and happening to say so to my rector he said he wished someone would write a poem on the subject.[20]

Perhaps Hopkins saw a portrait of himself in these nuns who had to leave their homeland as outlaws because of their Catholic faith. In a nun's reputed cry, "O Christ, Christ, come quickly," he saw the courage and heroism he had valued all his life. What Hopkins produced was not only a memorial of these nuns and their tragic death, but a testimony to his own religious life. Hopkins' poem, "The Wreck of the Deutschland," is the most autobiographical of all his works, as well as the most complex and demanding in its use of new rhythms and word combinations. It was no wonder that his poet friend, later poet laureate, Robert Bridges, called it the "dragon in the gate," barring the way to the rest of his poetry. The poem, like almost everything he wrote, was never accepted for publication, not even in the Jesuit journal *Month*—probably because of its complexity.

In this poem and those that followed, Hopkins' priestly and poetic vocations *seemed,* at least on the surface, to come together. All the poems he wrote as a priest were written in the spirit of the Jesuit motto *Ad Majorem Dei Gloriam*, "For the Greater Glory of God." Poems that praise the glory of God throughout all creation, and especially in minute particularities, followed in rapid succession. "These things, these things were here and but the beholder / Wanting," he said in "Hurrahing in Harvest," and his poetry literally became a *witness* to God's glory in the world. One night, as he looked out of his window at St. Beuno's, he saw the moon rising over the hill of Maenefa, and wrote "Moonrise June 19, 1876":

> This was the prized, the desirable sight,
>   unsought, presented so easily,
> Parted me leaf and leaf, divided me, eyelid and
>   eyelid of slumber.

Still, Hopkins felt interiorly "divided" by the two vocations that for him seemed to be in conflict. He continued to write poetry, but at times almost with a sense of guilt. Some of his greatest poetry—"God's Grandeur,"

"The Starlight Night," "The Lantern Out of Doors," "As Kingfishers Catch Fire," "Spring," "In the Valley of the Elwy," "The Windhover"—was written during this period of amazing fecundity while he was in Wales. Never again would such a happy confluence of place and peace exist, which would allow him such freedom of expression, or, as Hopkins himself would put it, "freedom of play."

Hopkins had expected to remain in Wales for four years to complete the course in theology. But his Jesuit examiners failed him in his oral exams at the end of his third year. He would have to go elsewhere: "Much against my inclination, I shall have to leave Wales," he wrote to Bridges.[21] Only recently has the reason for this brilliant student's failure come to light. Hopkins had become a follower of the fourteenth-century theologian, John Duns Scotus, whose awareness of the particularity of things— *haeceitas*—and humanism attracted him. Duns Scotus helped Hopkins find a philosophical underpinning for his experiential concept of inscape. He pressed the Scotist case too eagerly for his examiners, who were strict followers of Thomas Aquinas. As with so much else in his spiritual and intellectual life, Hopkins' devotion to Scotus was fully integrated into his way of seeing the world. He had written in his journal some years earlier: "At this time I had first begun to get hold of the copy of Scotus on the *Sentences* in the Baddely library and was flush with a new stroke of enthusiasm. It may come to nothing or it may be a mercy from God. But just then when I took in any inscape of the sky or sea I thought of Scotus."[22]

Hopkins paid dearly for deviating from his examiners' expectations. Although his failure did not jeopardize his ordination to the priesthood, he never achieved the status of a fully professed member by taking the "fourth vow" of solemn profession. Instead, he was designated a "spiritual co-adjutor." If he had been successful in his examination, he might well have taken up an important office in the Order such as a professorship, a position "well suited to his Oxford qualifications," as Father Christopher Devlin, S.J. points out.[23] Knowing he would have to leave St. Beuno's and his beloved Wales he began "Pied Beauty" with the words: *Ad Majorem Dei Gloriam.*"

He was ordained to the priesthood on September 23, 1877. From then on, Hopkins received his assignments in short order—nine in a three to four-year period. Is it any wonder that he called himself "Fortune's football"? During a ten-month assignment at Oxford as curate of St. Aloysius' church, he walked up Port Meadows only to find his beloved aspen trees "all felled." He wrote

"Binsey Poplars" to protest the encroachment of industrialism on the pastoral beauty of Oxford:

> My aspens dear, whose airy cages quelled,
> Quelled or quenched in leaves the leaping sun,
> All felled, felled, are all felled;

Throughout these years of abrupt dislocation, moving from one location to another, an ominous note of sadness and weariness—bodily and spiritual—began to sound in Hopkins' letters. From Sheffield, in 1878, he wrote to Bridges that "Life here is dank as ditchwater" and that he was "reduced to great weakness by diarrhea, which lasts too, as if I were poisoned."[24] We now know that he may have suffered from undiagnosed Crohn's disease, causing continual diarrhea, fatigue, and eyestrain. Hopkins also felt an unremitting sense of failure to accomplish anything of worth. The industrial, urban settings to which he was assigned gave him little inspiration and certainly added to his sense of gloom. He could no longer even see the sun much less any other of nature's beauties. He found Liverpool the "most museless" of places, and with his charge of parish work—discharged with little success—he had almost no time for writing of any kind, either poetry or letters. One day, while walking home from a country house near Liverpool where he had celebrated the Eucharist for the family of a young girl named Margaret, he wrote "Spring and Fall: *to a young child*." The poem addresses the young girl, asking if she grieves over the "unleaving" of the woods, and it ends with the lines:

> It ís the blight man was born for,
> It is Margaret you mourn for.

By the end of the poem, the woods' "unleaving" has become a metaphor for all of life's leave-takings, and especially the final one: death, which will come even to this lively young girl. As his sense of frustration and failure grew, he wrote the poem, "Peace," just as he was about to leave Oxford, asking: "When will you ever, Peace, wild wooddove, shy wings shut, / Your round me roaming end, and under be my boughs?" Peace, like this wild bird, had eluded Hopkins in his many journeys.

Hopkins experienced some relief in 1881 when he arrived at Roehampton, London for his "tertianship," a kind of second novitiate. He resolved again not to write any poetry, but would *vacare Deo* (be empty for God). Once more, the discord he felt between writing poetry and his "true" vocation to the priesthood can be detected in this resolution.

I cannot in conscience spend time on poetry, neither have I the inducements and inspirations that make others compose. Feeling, love in particular, is the great moving power and spring of verse and the only person that I am in love with seldom, especially now, stirs my heart sensibly and when he does I cannot always "make capital" of it, it would be a sacrilege to do so.[25]

To Dixon, who so admired his poetry and tried to get it published, Hopkins replied that he must "make a sacrifice of hopes of fame."[26] To which Dixon wisely responded, "Surely one vocation cannot destroy another; and such a Society as yours will not remain ignorant that you have such gifts as have seldom been given by God to man."[27] It does not appear that Dixon's arguments were persuasive. Though the ten-month stay at Manresa House offered him some respite, by August 1882, when Hopkins had taken up his next assignment teaching classics to young Jesuits at Stonyhurst College, he was saying again that in all likelihood, he would never do anything lasting.

Tragically, measured against the heroism of the Jesuit ideal—a courageous "knight of the cross" fighting for souls, waging a spiritual warfare of service and sacrifice under the standard of Christ[28]—Hopkins always felt himself a failure. Heroism composed of great deeds—preaching, teaching, or service—was not to be his. This poet, who had proclaimed, "What I do is me, for that I came," found his doings "broken off undone" at every turn. The real war he waged was the "war within." In his vocation to the priesthood, he too was, as he said of Christ, "doomed to succeed by failure."[29]

It was only toward the end of his life that Hopkins found another model of sainthood in St. Alphonsus Rodriguez, a Jesuit lay brother who merely "watched the door"; the example of this saint's life allowed Hopkins to forge for himself another kind of valor.

In honour of
St. Alphonsus Rodriguez
Laybrother of the Society of Jesus

Honour is flashed off exploit, so we say;
And those strokes once that gashed flesh or
    galled shield
Should tongue that time now, trumpet now that
    field,
And, on the fighter, forge his glorious day.
On Christ they do and on the martyr may;
But be the war within, the brand we wield
Unseen, the heroic breast not outward-steeled,
Earth hears no hurtle then from fiercest fray.

> Yet God (that hews mountain and continent,
> Earth, all, out; who, with trickling increment,
> Veins violets and tall trees makes more and
>   more)
> Could crowd career with conquest while there
>   went
> Those years and years by of world without event
> That in Majorca Alfonso watched the door.

If God's creative energies could hew mountains and vein violets, they could certainly make saints not only of great heroes but also of ordinary doorkeepers and perhaps of those who, like Hopkins, feel their lives are useless. Like St. Alphonsus Rodriguez, the Jesuit brother whom the Church had just canonized in 1887, Hopkins merely got to "watch the door," to be the gatekeeper by grading hundreds of entrance examinations for students who were matriculating in the classics at University College, Dublin. For Hopkins, as for St. Alphonsus Rodriguez, "Honour was [not] flashed off exploit." Hopkins remembered that a priest once said: "a great part of life to the holiest of men consists in the well performance...of ordinary duties," and he observed: "And this comforted against the thought of the little I do in the way of hard penances."[30] His tendency to ascetic practices had been tempered by the hard reality of his illness and weariness and in that respect, he was similar to a contemporary of his, St. Thérèse of Lisieux, who wanted to follow the path of St. Joan of Arc, but whose circumstances afforded her the "little way." Perhaps Hopkins' true vocation was to "watch the door," to live the simple, unacknowledged life of a contemplative poet/priest. In his failure to be a hero in the usual sense, he succeeded in realizing a contemplative heroism.

In a way he could not foresee, Hopkins indeed became a doorkeeper through his poetry, opening doors to the sacred, for those of us searching for God and for meaning amid the chaos of the world. The doors he opened were opened onto eternity.

Hopkins finally received a permanent appointment in 1884, to a place where, sadly, he felt more alienated than ever: Dublin. Even before his arrival, he was aware of an "Irish row" over his appointment as the newly elected Fellow of the now Jesuit Royal University of Ireland. Some on the university Senate, including Cardinal McCabe, wanted to grant the position to an Irishman. The Cardinal thought "this place had had too much of Englishmen in its past history," while Father William

Delaney, the University President, thought English Jesuits would be better qualified.[31] Father Tuite, the Jesuit provincial of Ireland, had already warned Delaney that staffing his college with foreign Jesuits would only add to the failure of Cardinal Newman's Catholic University in Ireland. Unwittingly, Hopkins stepped into the centuries-old conflict between the English and the Irish. To the end of his life, Hopkins felt employed (he never said by whom), in the "unlawful" cause of the Irish patriots against England. Although he had sympathy for the plight of the Irish, as with the poor in general, he never reconciled that sympathy with his antipathy toward their cause. He was never at home in Dublin, and knew none of the Jesuits of the Irish Province. "Dublin itself is a joyless place," he wrote to Bridges, though he had expected it to be otherwise. His 1885 poem, "To Seem the Stranger," captures his sense of estrangement from family, country, and even Christ:

> To seem the stranger lies my lot, my life
> Among strangers.   Father and mother dear,
> Brothers and sisters are in Christ not near
> And he my peace my parting, sword and strife.

My Winter World

Founded by Newman, the Catholic Royal University of Dublin was now run by the Jesuits. It occupied dilapidated buildings on St. Stephen's Green and was so strapped for money that it had no real library. Hopkins lived in one of the two buildings, which was, as Hopkins put it, "a sort of ruin." From his small room on the third floor he could look out on a little patch of desolate lawn. At the time, St. Stephen's Green was more of a dumping ground than a park. Yet, he could write to Newman that he continued to see the hand of Providence in the events that brought him to Ireland, though he could not lift his spirits there. Instead, he sank into a deep depression.

Out of this blackness, the "heart of darkness," which was for Hopkins a dark night of the soul, he wrote his "terrible sonnets," six poems that narrate Hopkins' inner agony in heart-breaking detail. These poems of desolation: "Carrion Comfort," "No worst, there is none," "To seem the stranger," "I wake and feel the fell of dark, not day," "My own heart let me more have pity on," and "Thou art indeed just, Lord," came, said Hopkins, "like inspirations unbidden and against my will."[32] Yet, still in the desolation of this night, he was able to write the hopeful poem, "That Nature Is a Heraclitean Fire and of the

Comfort of the Resurrection." The brilliance of this poem's "immortal diamond" shines through, but does not blot out the darkness of the "terrible sonnets." In some way they are all prayers released from the lowest register of the human soul.

Hopkins dragged on in Ireland for five more years. His only relief was the brief holidays he spent at Monasterevan, County Kildare, with the Cassidys, an Irish family loyal to England. During his last retreat in January 1889, he called himself a "straining eunuch,"[33] and in March wrote the poem, "Thou art indeed just, Lord, if I contend with Thee," which ends with the lines, "birds build—but not I build; no, but strain / Time's eunuch, and not breed one work that wakes. / Mine, O thou lord of life, send my roots rain." Just before his final illness, he wrote his last poem, an apology for the loss of his inspiration and creativity, which he addressed to Bridges:

> O then if in my lagging lines you miss
> The roll, the rise, the carol, the creation,
> My winter world, that scarcely breathes that bliss
> Now, yields you, with some sighs, our explanation.

Hopkins' final illness and death from typhoid fever was probably brought on by his chronic weakness and the extremely unsanitary condition of the college, where rats were found in the uninspected drains.[34] In the last letter he was able to write his family, he expressed relief to be free of his duties:

> My sickness falling at the most pressing time of the University work, there will be the devil to pay. Only there is no harm in saying, that gives *me* no trouble but an unlooked for relief. At many such a time I have been in a sort of extremity of mind, now I am the placidest soul in the world.[35]

Hopkins died at age 44 on June 8, 1889; on his deathbed he was heard to say, "I am so happy; I am so happy." The many years of personal grieving and professional futility were over, and he could now give himself up to the God he had in fact served so well.

During a retreat in 1883, Hopkins had written that he "earnestly asked our Lord to watch over my compositions...that he should have them as his own and employ or not employ them as he should see fit. And this I believe is heard."[36] He once told Bridges that he would leave his poems in the hands of Providence, but asked him to be their executor. Thirty years later, in 1918, Bridges published the entire body of works his fellow poet had entrusted to him over the many years of their friendship. A sort of divine irony hangs over the eventual vindication of Hopkins' genius; all those who failed to publish or appreciate him in his lifetime have passed into insignificance while the greatness of this humble poet lives on.

Chapter 3

Priest and Poet

His Other Writings

JOURNALS

While Hopkins did not actually have much of his work published in his lifetime, he wrote a great deal; and though he began many projects, he did so only to abandon them. Perhaps the most representative of his writings were his journals, which he kept most of his life. These journals reveal a keen observer of nature who possessed an equally keen love of language. Hopkins' many notes on the origins and meanings of words (e.g., "*Flit, vol-are, volit-are, fleet,* to *fleet, flight, flutter, flitter,* etc.*") were certainly a preparation for the amazing word play of his poems. His exploration of sounds and etymologies indicate that words had almost the power of an incantation for him. His journals also demonstrate an appreciation of the natural scene in which religious awe often mixes with careful description: "As we drove home the stars came out thick: I leant back to look at them and my heart opening more than usual praised our Lord to and in whom all that beauty comes home,"[1] and "I do not think I have ever seen anything more beautiful than the blue-bell I have been looking at. I know the beauty of our Lord by it."[2] He delighted in the intricacies and variety of nature to the point of astonishment. He who once exclaimed, "What is the world? It is a poem of beauty," God's script read in nature. He loved the way God had written wildness into the beauties of nature.

Hopkins' journals and early diaries reveal a contemplative in the making. He is everywhere the great observer, recording minutely detailed descriptions of clouds and trees and flowers. Images found in the journals will be distilled and finely honed later in his poems: there are "pied skies," "brindled and hatched scaping of cloud," "cobalt blue poured on the hills," "wonderful downpour of leaf." But the element which makes a person truly contemplative—letting the mystery of it all surprise one with wonder and joy and delight—begins to blossom in his journals.

LETTERS AND ESSAYS

Hopkins' letters to family and friends have been collected in three volumes that are full of gems—patient explanations of his poems and profound insights into his religious faith. Unpublished essays written at Oxford as well as lectures for his brief teaching assignments at

Roehampton and Stonyhurst continue to supply insights into his amazing breadth of genius and poetic expression.

Like Jessica Powers, Hopkins had his own personal lexicon, but, like so much else that was "original, spare, strange," in this poet, many of his words were coined by him to capture and communicate his unique experience. The words particular to Hopkins' aesthetic vocabulary which recur throughout his writings, were "inscape," "instress," and "bidding." Other theological words that had a special meaning for him were "incarnation" and *"kenosis."* Each word may be considered as a theme running through Hopkins' writings. We can enrich our understanding and praying of his poetry by giving attention to them.

Inscape

If poetry means creating something new in the world—a new way of seeing and relating to reality—then Hopkins' poetry does this superbly. He invented a new term for his particular experience of the world and his shaping of that experience through poetry. The Greek root, *skopein,* means, "to look attentively." His own word, "inscape," includes the element of seeing a thing in all its distinctiveness, whatever makes it most itself. Thomas Aquinas might have referred to this distinction as the *essence of a thing,* but for Hopkins inscape embraced a thing's unique physical attributes as well as its innermost being. Hopkins had a keen sense that everyone should be able to attain this experience. In his journal of 1872, he wrote, "I thought how sadly beauty of inscape was unknown and buried away from simple people and yet how near at hand it was if they had eyes to see it and it could be called out everywhere again."[3] Because the inscape of a thing imparted its beauty and holiness, Hopkins suffered "a great pang" whenever he saw things destroyed, such as the poplars cut down.

To his friend and fellow Catholic poet, Coventry Patmore, he offered an explanation of inscape that sounds like the definition of sacrament:

> It is certain that in nature outward beauty is the proof of inward beauty, outward good of inward good. Fineness, proportion of feature comes from a moulding force, which succeeds in asserting itself over the resistance of cumbersome or restraining matter.[4]

If sacrament is the outward form of inward grace, then each thing, in its inscape—its "inward good" evidenced by "outward good"—is much like a sacrament of nature. Far from a merely banal experience of "landscape," Hopkins' inscape is a moment of grace, a fleeting vision of the world transfigured. The experience of inscape took him deeper into what we might call the "soul" of things and persons, but not in any dualistic sense. To say the world is inscaped by God is to say with Psalm 19, "The heavens declare the glory of God." Hopkins knew God's "glory," the Old Testament idea of *kabod*, as almost a physical, shining presence, a radiance of the light of God breaking through ordinary things—the kingfisher's fire, the dragonfly's flame, the shining from shook foil. In "Hurrahing in Harvest," he can say:

> I walk, I lift up, I lift up heart, eyes,
> > Down all that *glory* in the heavens to glean
> > our Saviour;

Hopkins believed inscape could be discovered anywhere: "All the world is full of inscape and chance left free to act falls into an order as well as purpose: looking out of my window I caught it in the random clods and broken heaps of snow made by the cast of a broom."[5] His fellow Jesuits remembered him intently studying the patterns of frost in a mud puddle. Inscape cannot be imposed on matter by the mind; it is matter's gift to us when we are able to receive it in contemplation. This ability to discover inscape everywhere meant that even the darkest events divulged the hand of God. In "The Wreck of the Deutschland" Hopkins found inscape in the apparently meaningless death of the German nuns on England's shore. He discovered the distinctive inscape of his own self and wrote of it in his commentary on St. Ignatius' *Spiritual Exercises:*

> I find myself both as man and as myself something most determined and distinctive, at pitch, more distinctive and higher pitched than anything else I see...that taste of myself...which is more distinctive than the taste of ale or alum. Nothing else in nature comes near this unspeakable stress of pitch, distinctiveness, and selving, this selfbeing of my own.[6]

He believed the purpose of his poetry was to convey this experience of inscape: "as air, melody is what strikes me most of all in music and design in painting, so design, pattern or what I am in the habit of calling 'inscape' is what I above all aim at in poetry."[7] This distinctive pattern or pitch revealing inner depths is evident everywhere in his poetry. He speaks of inscape in poetic lines such as "the dearest freshness deep down things"; "Self flashes off frame and face"; "head, heart, hand, heel, and shoulder / ...beat and breathe in power."

But inscape is also unity where it is least expected: unity hidden within the diversity or "piedness" of his poems; it is the wholeness hidden in their diversity of images and sounds. Hopkins' experience of inscape resembles Thomas Merton's "hidden wholeness" at the heart of things, but adds a certain quirkiness, involving an integrity of form, of inner and outer content. For Hopkins, inscape involved both the unique, unrepeatable design of a thing and its own inner beauty shining forth. We might say inscape meant seeing holiness manifested through beauty, seeing the "grandeur of God" shining out from creation in an epiphanic vision.

Instress

As in everything he saw Hopkins experienced what he called "inscape," so its effect on him he called "instress." If inscape was *what* Hopkins experienced in nature and human beings, *instress* was *how* he experienced it. Instress is that "charge" between things and us; that "stem of stress," as he called it, that communicates the world's inscape to us. In his personal journals and his essays, Hopkins created a language for contemplation, calling it in effect the *instress of inscape*. Perhaps today, using the language of quantum physics, Hopkins would talk about instress in terms of the currents of quantum energy connecting all life and being. Hopkins put it beautifully in his notes on the *Spiritual Exercises:*

All things, therefore, are charged with love, are charged with God, and if we know how to touch them give off sparks and take fire, yield drops and flow, ring and tell of him.[8]

We too can be charged with the light and power of God "if we know how to touch," how to be instressed by the things of this earth. In his instress of inscape, Hopkins experienced what another Jesuit, Pierre Teilhard de Chardin, was to describe years later:

> This scintillation of diverse beauties was so complete, so captivating, and also so swift that I felt it touch and penetrate all my powers simultaneously, so that the very core of my being vibrated in response to it, sounding a unique note of expansion and happiness...[9]

With instress, the poet is stamped or stressed by the inscape, "My heart in hiding stirred for a bird, —the achieve of, the mastery of the thing!"[10] Instress is our capacity to receive and respond to a vision or to the poem, which conveys it. Instress is surprise, awe, astonishment, and even an ecstatic joy. Its surprise is the kind that comes only from contact with the otherness of God. In true ecstasy (*ecs-stasis*), we stand outside ourselves not indulging our own will and desires and not trying to master the experience with our idea of what it should be.

"Crushed. Why do men then now not reck his rod?"

Because he allowed himself to be instressed by the things of the world, Hopkins experienced the present moment as eternal, matter as spirit, and all things as charged with God. A poem is the stressing (expression) of the poet's instress (experience). As the poet says in Part I of "The Wreck":

> Since, tho' he is under the world's splendour
>   and wonder,
> His mystery must be instressed, stressed;
> For I greet him the days I meet him, and bless
>   when I understand.

Though inscape manifests God's presence in nature as it does in the poem, its stress on us must first be experienced—that is, instressed. Instress speaks of the transforming power of God in each natural thing and in persons. With regard to God—and in Hopkins everything holds this regard—we might call instress "grace." We can be instressed by the inscapes of the whole world, and thus we can experience God's grace in all things.

In an unfinished poem, perhaps written around the same time as the "terrible sonnets," Hopkins expresses beautifully his role as poet in being instressed by God and emphasizing it:

Thee God I come from, to thee go,
All day long I like fountain flow
From thy hand out, swayed about
Mote-like in thy mighty glow.

What I know of thee I bless,
As acknowledging thy *stress*
On my being and as seeing
Something of thy holiness.

Hopkins allows himself to flow out from God's being, and thus God's stress on him occurs; his part is to acknowledge, to "bless" God's stress on his life. His complete attunement to God in the first stanza gives way in the second to a deliberate assent to God's grace. Hopkins' poems were those assents, those acknowledgments of what had by then become an unconscious agreement—a flowing out—with God. He brought the continual surprise of instress into his poems. In language and imagery, in surprising turns of phrase and irregular rhythms, and in word-creations, Hopkins communicates this instress to his readers.

Bidding

As with any idea that meant a great deal to him, Hopkins invented his own word for the way a poem should address his reader. He understood the poem's *bidding* as:

[T]he art or virtue of saying everything right *to* or *at* the hearer, interesting him, holding him in the attitude of correspondent or addressed or at least concerned, making it everywhere an act of intercourse—and of discarding everything that does not bid, does not tell.[11]

Bidding entails an offer, a request, an invitation, even a command to the hearer to engage with his poems directly. More than a century later, Hopkins' poems still "bid" for our attention, sometimes explicitly with words like "look," "pray," "bid," and "buy." In "the Starlight Night," he exclaims: "Buy then! bid then!—What?—Prayer, patience, alms, vows." This poem is a direct request for us to "bid" for the beauty and wonder of the starry night with our prayerful attention and our "alms," our willingness to give away any accumulation of wealth or possessions, which stand in the way of our seeing. Implicitly, all of his poems make this request. Just as Jesus bid his followers to "have ears to hear" (Mk 4:9), Hopkins, perhaps anticipating how increasingly difficult this would become, tells us to hear. Most of all, Hopkins' poems bid us to pray.

Incarnation

It would hardly be possible to overestimate the importance of the Incarnation for this poet. For Hopkins the whole world *was* the incarnation (literally "becoming flesh") of Christ, and his own life had become one small part of that greater event.

> All that happens in Christendom and so in the whole world affected, marked, as a great seal, and like any other historical event, and in fact more than any other event, by the Incarnation.... But our lives and in particular those of religious, as mine, not only inwardly but most visibly and outwardly, shaped by Christ's. Without that even outwardly the world could be so different that we cannot even guess it. And my life is determined by the Incarnation down to most of the details of the day.[12]

This is an apt summary of a life penetrated to its marrow with the reality that the Word *was made flesh and dwelt among us*. The Incarnation became the inward and outward shape—the inscape—of Hopkins' life. For Hopkins, the Incarnation of the divine took place not only once in history, but takes place throughout all of nature and within all beings created to give God praise: "For Christ plays in ten thousand places, / Lovely in limbs, and lovely in eyes not his" as he proclaims in his "Kingfishers" poem. Christ incarnates himself over and over in the world of nature and in human beings, becoming their inscape or individuating design.

Attempting to explain the mystery of the Incarnation to Robert Bridges, an unbeliever, Hopkins remarked that "to some people this is a 'dogma,' a word they almost chew, that is an equation in theology, the dull algebra of schoolmen; to others it is news of their dearest friend or friends...their knowledge leaves their minds swinging; poised but on the quiver. And this might be the ecstasy of interest."[13] The Incarnation was the "ecstasy of interest" in Hopkins' whole life and endeavor; he was moved by such ecstasy in his vision of the world and his vocation to live Christ. This ecstasy enabled Hopkins to see Christ in the "least of these"—the earth and its dappled things, workmen, stones, bells.

Incarnation may be the most pervasive idea in Hopkins' life and work, the lens through which he saw the world:

> God's utterance of himself in himself is God the
> Word, outside himself is this world. This world then
> is word, expression, news of God. Therefore its end,
> its purpose, its purport, its meaning, is God and its
> life or work to name and praise him.[14]

In effect, the incarnation became the very principle that gave shape to Hopkins' poetry. Hopkins worked at a union of form and content in his poetry that mirrored the union of Word and flesh, spirit and matter. His poetry incarnates the Word, Christ, in the flesh of its form: "to recognize the form you are employing and to mean it is everything."[15] The naturalness of his sprung rhythm combines with his images and syntax to elevate the verse. The effect, then, is one of grace building on nature. What he says about his sonnet on Henry Purcell, the composer he loved, could be considered his incarnational method: "while he is aiming only at impressing me his hearer with the meaning in hand, I am looking out meanwhile for his specific, his individual markings and mottlings, 'the sakes of him.'"

Hopkins' own interpretation of the doctrine of the Incarnation accents not only Christ's union of two natures, human and divine, but with the whole material, physical world as well. In Hopkins' theology, Christ's Incarnation is directly linked to creation rather than being an aftermath of the Fall and an act of atonement to God. Christ becomes incarnated in created matter, making matter itself holy, and for no reason other than God the Father's abundant love and God the Son's responding love.

It follows, then, that for Hopkins, Christ's body inscapes the world as Eucharist. It consecrates all matter, all of the earth, all of the universe, just as the bread and wine are consecrated in the celebration of the Eucharist to become Christ's body and blood. The universe is holy. In light of this fundamental reality, Hopkins can proclaim ever more emphatically that the world is "charged with the grandeur of God" and that "Christ plays in ten thousand places." The Incarnation of Christ guarantees matter's inscape, its inner goodness, and its loveliness.

The Great Sacrifice

Hopkins' sacramental view of reality reminds us of Teilhard de Chardin's "Mass over the World," where, alone in the desert without elements with which to offer the Eucharist, he consecrates the whole earth as the bread and its sufferings as the chalice of wine. Hopkins saw the Incarnation as "the great sacrifice," and his own life bore witness to this aspect as well. In a spiritual essay, "Creation and Redemption: The Great Sacrifice," written during the Long Retreat of 1881, he replies to the question why the Son of God went forth from the Father. He says it was "To give God glory and that by sacrifice, sacrifice offered in the barren wilderness outside of God.... The sacrifice would be the Eucharist."[16]

He also understood Christ's human, historical Incarnation as a sacrifice of all worldly success:

Above all, Christ our Lord: his career was cut short and, whereas he would have wished to succeed by success—for it is insane to lay yourself out for failure...
—nevertheless he was doomed to succeed by failure; his plans were baffled, his hopes dashed, and his work was done by being broken off undone.[17]

The antitheses of success and failure, hope and despair, unity and disunity certainly apply to the poet's own life.

Kenosis

In its emphasis on sacrifice, Hopkins' incarnational theology stresses one more element that should be mentioned—the *kenosis* or self-emptying of Christ.[18] *Kenosis* is no casual theological term in Hopkins' repertoire, it rather is a principle pervading every aspect of his life and work. When speaking aesthetically, Hopkins called it "surprise" or instress; in his more religious reflections, he drew on the example of Christ, referring to his *"kenosis"* or emptying. He wrote an exegesis of the famous passage underlying this doctrine in Philippians 2:5–11 for Bridges:

Christ's life and character are such as appeal to all the world's admiration, but there is one insight St. Paul gives us of it which is very secret and seems to me more touching and constraining than everything else is:

70

[F]inding, as in the first instant of his incarnation he did, his human nature informed by the godhead—he thought it nevertheless no snatching-matter for him to be equal with God, but annihilated himself, taking the form of servant;...he emptied or exhausted himself so far as that was possible, of godhead.[19]

Kenosis, or what Hopkins calls "the great sacrifice" is the necessary precondition for the reality of Incarnation. "It was only through Christ and the great sacrifice that God had meant any being to come to him at all."[20] That Hopkins saw this *kenosis* as a paradigm for his own existence is made clear in the same letter to Bridges:

It is this holding of himself back, and not snatching at the truest and highest good, the good that was his right, nay his possession from a past eternity in his other nature, his own being and self, which seems to me the root of all his holiness and the imitation of this the root of all moral good in other men.[21]

Hopkins practiced this ideal of *kenosis* in his own life and in the creating of his poetry. His decision to destroy his poetry and no longer write betrayed a *kenosis* even of "the good that was his right."[22] Allowing himself to be instressed in the face of nature's inscapes necessitated a self-emptying of his desires and an assent to nature in all its otherness. To receive the vision of what really is there and not what we want or imagine to be there requires self-emptying.

CHAPTER 4

Praying with the Sonnets

I f we want to prepare ourselves to pray with the poems of Gerard Manley Hopkins, a good place to begin is with the Psalter. The range and depth of feeling found in Hopkins' poems—from the heights of exultation to the depths of desperation—can be compared with the Psalms. Through the centuries, both Jews and Christians have turned to the psalms as their prayer book, an invitation to open their hearts to God. Hopkins' poems resemble the psalms in their intensity of emotion as well as in their barrage of rapidly shifting images and their parallelisms.

The first thing to acknowledge in reading Hopkins' poems is their difficulty. They are challenging both poetically and religiously: poetically because Hopkins experimented with every aspect of poetry—diction (word choices), syntax (word order), and rhythm or meter. Nearly all of his completed poems are sonnets. Yet, even when he chose the sonnet form with its regular number of syllables and lines, he experimented with it, sometimes shortening or lengthening the number of lines and adding any number of syllables. He did not mind and actually expected that the meaning of his poems would at first be obscure. He believed that on repeated readings, they would "explode" on the reader, as he told Bridges:

> One of two kinds of clearness one should have—
> either the meaning to be felt without effort as fast
> as one reads or else, if dark at first reading, when
> once made out *to explode*."[1]

Many of his poems are indeed "dark at first reading." He expected a great deal of his readers, and perhaps that is why he had so few during his lifetime. They were not ready for him.

Hopkins' poems challenge us even more at the religious level. While a Jesuit, nearly everything he wrote employed religious imagery in subtle and not so subtle ways. Christ is the explicit or implicit center of all his mature poems, just as Christ was the model of Hopkins' own life and the lens through which he viewed the world. Bridges, sometimes Anglican and sometimes agnostic, felt discomfort with the overtly religious quality of Hopkins' poetry. Hopkins' poems are so thoroughly *incarnational* that we can no more separate the word from the body of the poems than we can ignore their materiality in their meaning. Matter and spirit, word and flesh, form and content belong inextricably together. They cannot be reduced to "either/or's," but sustain the union of the Catholic "both/and," as Karl Barth once called it.

However, in recognizing the difficulty of reading Hopkins' poems, we are in good company. Hopkins knew that only after a generation or more would people begin to grasp his poetry, so complex were its innovations. In a sense, then, he wrote it for us. Because we now have the benefit of several generations of commentaries on his poetry, we can appreciate it more.

The very difficulty in reading his poetry may seem an obstacle to prayer. Yet, I believe this very fact leads us away from the danger of a banal, merely superficial prayer and into a deeper prayer of the heart. In his poetry, Hopkins expresses certain recurrent ideas, which may be grouped into categories according to themes that I am taking from significant phrases he used in his poetry, namely "Dappled Things," "Handsome Hearts," "Christ at Play," and "Time's Eunuch." These phrases reflect Hopkins' love for the infinite varieties of creation, for the beauty of character in human beings, and for the universality of the Incarnation in created nature and human beings. They also reflect Hopkins' personal struggle with the "dark night of the soul."

Perhaps because Hopkins' poetry requires such attentiveness, as well as repeated readings, the method of *lectio divina* is especially appropriate for praying his poetry. We will follow the stages of this method by 1) reading attentively and slowly; 2) reflecting thoughtfully; 3) posing questions that lead us into prayer; and 4) praying the poetry. The following reflections on selected poems within each category include thoughtful explorations and questions intended to open up each poem for prayer.

Dappled Things

This theme, "dappled things," comes from "Pied Beauty," a poem that can be considered almost a metaphor for poetry in general, and in particular, for Hopkins' poetry.

Pied Beauty

Glory be to God for dappled things—
  For skies of couple-colour as a brinded cow;
    For rose-moles all in stipple upon trout
      that swim;
Fresh-firecoal chestnut-falls; finches' wings;
  Landscape plotted and pieced—fold, fallow,
      and plough;
    And áll trádes, their gear and tackle and trim.

All things counter, original, spare, strange;
  Whatever is fickle, freckled (who knows how?)
    With swift, slow; sweet, sour; adazzle, dim;
  He fathers-forth whose beauty is past change:
                Praise him.

Hopkins glorifies God not for what is most obviously
and conventionally beautiful, but for the "dappled,"
mottled, speckled, freckled things of life. Those things
which are "pied"—with blemishes that some might say
mar the purity and perfection of a cow, a fish, a finch—
that he celebrates in this poem. He rejoices in the diversity of things of "couple-colour" found in both the ani-
mal and the human worlds: the cows "pied" in stark black
and white, trout "stippled" with tiny rose dots, as Impres-
sionist painters stippled, daubing/dappling their pictures,
chestnuts falling off trees like a rain of red coals, the
motley wings of finches, and "áll trádes" of peoples. The
first stanza zooms in on *haecceitas* of particular things, their
very special *thisness* or being. The second stanza performs
a cosmic sweep of creation, with all its ambiguities and
contrarieties. The things Hopkins includes in the poem
are all somewhat quirky and odd in themselves—remarkable in their individuality and together making up a patchwork quilt or multicolored collage.

We human beings belong to this ever-changing variety of creation, to "áll trádes" of peoples with their array of "gear and tackle and trim," their own distinguishing marks or inscapes. We are equally "dappled" in our diversity of occupations and appearance. The line "All things counter, original, spare, strange" is inclusive of life's tumbles and surprises. Even all things that "counter," that is, oppose, each other, are under God's all-embracing care and creation. The lion and the lamb, the powerful and the weak, the rich and the poor are all given life by one Creative Spirit. God loves variety, says the poet, and that variety, even in its motleyness, is beautiful to God, gives God glory, and is reflective of God's unchanging, yet ever expanding beauty.

Hopkins wrote "Pied Beauty" toward the end of his time at St. Beuno's, nestled among the Welsh hills and valleys. I have been there and can testify to the magnificent beauty of the lush green landscape of the Valley of the Clywd spreading out under billowy white clouds that seem in their enormity to embrace the earth. It is no wonder that this place so inspired Hopkins, a place where he found a variegated beauty, which corresponded to his passion for seeing. The play of light and shadow across the "landscape plotted and pieced" of the Valley of the

Clywd becomes a metaphor for all change. Hopkins combines a simple, uncomplicated statement of praise for God's glory that is found in out-of-the-way places with a more subtle reflection on the contradictions God has engendered there. This is not a conventionally pious affirmation of God's presence, but the expression of a faith that acknowledges the conflicts and contradictions of existence. Hopkins wrote this poem at a time when he personally experienced such contradictions—that of being denied a fourth year in Wales. There is nothing remarkable or pretty in a romantic sense here. In the remote and contradictory places, one must *look* for the beauty.

The following section is meant as a springboard for the reader to enter into a more prayerful relationship with this poem. The questions posed are intended to stimulate further questions and prayerful responses on the part of the reader.

For prayerful pondering

Although the poet casts his gaze far afield to search out the "dappled things," in order to pray with the poem, we might begin by applying it to ourselves and our world's "dappledness." Our lives are often as fickle and freckled, full of change and inner and outer contradictions. How often do I actually recognize and accept my life's "fickleness"? Am I willing to look into my "dim" corners, taste the "sour" flavors in my day, wait for the "slow" turn of events in my life? And what can I do with this new sight? What in my life is "counter" and how do I deal with this reality? How can I learn to accept and even to glorify God for the differences that are written so deeply in my life and world?

Any Jesuit or individual who makes a retreat with St. Ignatius' *Spiritual Exercises* learns to practice a holy indifference or "equanimity" toward good and bad fortune, to "neither desire nor even prefer to have riches rather than poverty, to seek honor rather than dishonor, to have a long life rather than a short one."[2] "Pied Beauty" calls us to embrace life's contradictions, its "swift, slow; sweet, sour; adazzle, dim" moments, because all of this diversity is included in God's "fathering" of creation.

From the intimately examined list of individual dappled things in the first stanza, we turn our gaze to a broader scene, one that includes the human cultivation of nature:

Landscape plotted and pieced—fold, fallow, and plough;

Here the varicolored patchwork spreads over the entire view; everything is dappled, "plotted and pieced," like the geometric designs seen from the window of an airplane as it takes off or descends, or like the patterns of a stained-glass window. This is Hopkins' view from the hill at St. Beuno's. If we were to speed up time, we would experience each stage of the land's cultivation: folding the ground under, leaving it fallow, and ploughing it again ("fold, fallow, and plough"). Our vision widens even further—to take in all human endeavors and the varieties of "gear and tackle and trim" of each occupation. How well do I accept the black and white, red and yellow dappledness of our increasingly multicultural society? Read through the lens of a postmodern world, Hopkins' poem suggests that the divisions and fault lines we tend to create—Catholic and Protestant, Jew and Christian and Muslim, white and black, with their differentiating "inscapes," are all part of a single overarching "landscape."

All things counter, original, spare, strange;

The poem moves toward an even greater universality and abstractness. Each of these adjectives introduces tension and ambiguity. Those things that are "counter" confront each other. Though we might wish for the harmony of Isaiah's prophecy: the "lion lying down with the lamb," this is not the reality we find in nature or human beings.

All things "original," and all things "spare"—set aside either because of excess or because they are specially saved or cared for—as well as all things "strange"—unfamiliar and divergent—are caught up in one of the two statements made. First, we can see "All things" (and the two lines that follow) as the object of the overarching subject:

He fathers-forth whose beauty is past change:

"He fathers-forth" all things. The verb "fathers-forth" establishes God's parental care and intimate relationship with all this variety and contrariety. Despite nature's changeableness, God's beauty is "past" or beyond change. But another statement occurs if we read the first part of this last tercet as subject: *"All things...Praise him."* Hopkins felt deeply that all created things praise God. In his notes on St. Ignatius' *Spiritual Exercises*, Hopkins describes the world as "a poem of beauty" which God has written, and asks: "What is it about? His praise, the reverence due him, the way to serve him; it tells him of his glory."[3] All things praise God by their very being, as the song of the three men in the fiery furnace expresses:

Bless the Lord, all the Lord's creation: praise and glorify him for ever! ...Let the earth bless the Lord: praise and glorify him for ever (Dan 3:57, 74).

Nature, in its particularities and entirety, reveals God. Nature is, as it were, a censer, lifting up the incense of praise. Hopkins headed his copy of the poem with the Jesuit motto: *Ad Majorem Dei Gloriam* ("For the greater glory of God") and ended it with the words, *Laus tibi Deus* ("Praise to God always"), making it indeed a prayer.

"Pied Beauty" moves through the world's variety, flux, and oppositions to a unity at its end. From the physical layout of the poem, we see how Hopkins placed the first and last lines ("Glory be to God...Praise him") on the page to give an almost physical appearance of God's enclosing a world full of contraries. God, whose beauty is past change, is the great reconciler of all these opposites. The reader experiences both the dappledness of all things, which praises the God who "fathers it forth." In either, "He fathers-forth [All things]" or "All things...Praise him," only mystery remains. We grapple with the One and the many, with multiplicity and unity. In a sense, this mystery is the essence of poetry.

God's Grandeur

The world is charged with the grandeur of God.
 It will flame out, like shining from shook foil;
 It gathers to a greatness, like the ooze of oil

Crushed.   Why do men then now not reck his
  rod?
Generations have trod, have trod, have trod;
    And all is seared with trade; bleared, smeared
        with toil;
    And wears man's smudge and shares
        man's smell: the soil
Is bare now, nor can foot feel, being shod.

And for all this, nature is never spent;
    There lives the dearest freshness deep down
        things;
And though the last lights off the black West went
    Oh, morning, at the brown brink eastward,
        springs—
Because the Holy Ghost over the bent
    World broods with warm breast and with ah!
        bright wings.

  Hopkins tells us that this poem is to be read "slowly,
strongly marking the rhythms and fetching out the syllables."[4] At this basic, "humble" level, one hears the
poem's sound-chimes, almost like the faint ringing of a
bell calling us to prayer. Word rhymes, scattered through-

out the poem, shine like stars in the night sky. In fact, Hopkins spoke of the rhymes of poetry—its alliterations (consonant rhymes), assonances (vowel rhymes), and other rhymes as their "brilliancy, starriness."[5] While we may not be conscious of such sound effects, they are working on us unconsciously and psychologically. For example, when we read this poem aloud, and "fetch out" the syllables of the first line, we hear the alliteration of the hard "g" sound "grandeur" and "God", as well as the softer "g" in "charged." The same hard "g" is repeated in the third line, as the poem in effect gathers the first and third line in speech, just as it does in meaning. All these sounds comprise what Hopkins called the "underthought" of the poem—its sounds and images and metaphors. The underthought literally underlies the "overthought," the explicit meaning of the poem. Even if the poem seems to be speaking of disunity, these word rhymes unify it, and when it speaks of unity and harmony, there may be subtle, underlying forces, like the sprung rhythm, breaking it apart. If we ignore this level in order to "get the meaning out of the poem," it is impossible to do justice to its full power.

For prayerful pondering
The world is charged with the grandeur of God.

"...of daylight's dauphin, dapple-dawn-drawn Falcon..."

We begin with an arresting image: "charged." This implies an electrical charge, a high voltage. The whole created world carries the energizing charge of God. If we say aloud the word "charged," and dwell on the image, we can begin to feel this current running through all life. "All things therefore," wrote Hopkins in his spiritual notes, "are charged with love, are charged with God, and if we know how to touch them, give off sparks and take fire, yield drops and flow, ring and tell of him."[6] "God's Grandeur" calls us to learn to "touch" the world so that we can know God in it. As in Jesuit spirituality, our "charge" or mission is to "see God in all things"— even in common tinsel or crushed oil. Hopkins audaciously chose the modern, "unpoetic" image of tinfoil to convey, through objects that seem unlikely, the dynamic presence and power of God. We can find God, implies the poem, even in our industrialized, technological society.

Yet, although God's grandeur charges up the world in the same way lightning might convey its charge to whatever it strikes, we human beings do not heed or "reck" God's lightning rod—an image Hopkins often used to speak of God the Father and Creator.

Hopkins then shifts to a question that must have been quite real for him, despite his previous celebration of God's presence in "shook foil": Why are we ruining the world God has given us and continues to charge? His answer simulates the "trodding" of generations over the earth by repeating the phrase "have trod, have trod, have trod." To the end of his life, Hopkins expressed dismay at the treading of trade over the earth. After living in or near cities in the north of England such as Liverpool, he wrote, "And our whole civilization is dirty, yea filthy, and especially in the north; for is it not dirty, yea filthy, to pollute the air...and the water?"[7] The Industrial Revolution of nineteenth-century England meant:

all is seared with trade; bleared, smeared with toil;

This searing of nature hints at today's terrible phrase, "scorched earth," which refers to nuclear holocaust. Hopkins, having breathed the "smoke-ridden air" around Sheffield and seen the first factories belching out black clouds across the skies, had an enormous sensitivity to "man's smudge" and "man's smell." This poem bids us to stop and consider what part, however small, we play in caring for the earth.

The poem's octave ends with a strong indictment and prophetic message:

the soil
Is bare now, nor can foot feel, being shod.

The very earth has become barren, and what is more, Hopkins believes we humans have become insensitive to this destruction. What began in the Garden of Eden, when *Adam* ("humans") became alienated from *adamah* ("the soil"), has become a total alienation of the human race from the earth. Can we take off our shoes, as did Moses, to stand on the earth's holy ground? Does our haste and greed to use the earth's goods and goodness for profit, prevent our reverencing it as charged with God's presence?

At this point, the bleak picture painted by the end of the poem's octave (first eight lines) abruptly shifts with the "And" that introduces the poem's sestet:

And for all this, nature is never spent.

Nature is never used up, never expended. Ultimately, it is not for sale; we cannot own or spend it. This line is followed by one of the most lilting in Hopkins' poetry:

There lives the dearest freshness deep down things.

At the heart of things, life's irrepressible if fragile growth burgeons beneath the surface. This "freshness"—

used as a noun to show its centrality—is really "dearest" in the sense of being most expensive and yet priceless; it cannot be bought, sold, or *spent*. The "dearest freshness" is really God's charge that can never be cut off.

Now the poem makes yet another surprising turn: from this simple acknowledgment of the world's indestructible life-force—a flowing out of the grandeur of God despite human efforts to destroy it—to the death and darkness that exist in the human and the natural worlds:

> **And though the last lights off the black West went**

Though our human hopes may go out, like the day's last light disappearing into descending darkness at sunset, another surprise awaits us:

> **Oh, morning at the brown brink eastward, springs—**

Morning always follows even our darkest night, as spring follows the deadest, coldest winter, because the Resurrection, revealing the blinding light of God's electric charge, rising out of the "brown," and no longer black sky as streaks of color with a coming dawn. The guarantee, we could say the guarantor, of this renewal, is the Holy Spirit, God's energy and power manifested to the world:

> **Because the Holy Ghost over the bent**
> **World broods with warm breast and with ah!**
> **bright wings.**

Like a Great Mother eagle, the Holy Ghost "broods," worries over her "brood" of fledglings, that are apt to follow their own "bent." She breeds and renews their life. She does this with "warm," comforting, and nurturing breast, and with "bright wings" lit by the ever-glowing flame of God. Light, love, warmth, and fire have the first and last word in this poem. While it has turned twice into the darkness: once of the sin of pollution, a moral evil; and once into the inevitably of death, a natural evil, all of these turns and twists are enclosed in God's power ("grandeur") and tenderness ("warm breast"). God's flaming out and gathering in have actually been occurring through the poet's use of a wide array of images and sounds, all "gathered to a greatness" by the poem itself, which imitates the all-embracing arms of the Mother God gathering her brood to her.

The poem's affirmations can become a source of questions, which we can bring to our praying of it. Do I still experience God's charge in the natural world? Do I know and cherish life's "dearest freshness"? Though I may go through the "black West" and "last lights" many times during my life—the end of a career, a relationship, a vision—how do I continue hoping for the dawn beyond? In what concrete ways do I work with the Holy Spirit's brooding for creative renewal in the human and natural worlds?

Christ's Play

Christ's centrality as the source and goal of all creation is the focus of much of Hopkins' mature poetry. Christ is the pivot of the poems. "As kingfishers catch fire" vividly embodies this play of Christ through all humanity. Hopkins never sent this untitled work to any of his friends, and it was found among his effects only after his death.

> As kingfishers catch fire, dragon flies dráw
>   fláme;
> As tumbled over rim in roundy wells
> Stones ring; like each tucked string tells, each
>   hung bell's
> Bow swung finds tongue to fling out broad its
>   name;
> Each mortal thing does one thing and the same:
> Deals out that being indoors each one dwells;
> Selves—goes itself; *myself* it speaks and spells,
> Crying *Whát I do is me: for that I came.*

Í say móre: the just man justices;
Kéeps gráce: thát keeps all his goings graces;
Acts in God's eye what in God's eye he is—
Chríst—for Christ plays in ten thousand places,
Lovely in limbs, and lovely in eyes not his
To the Father through the features of men's
        faces.

In this poem, Hopkins makes an elaborate series of comparisons, between all living things and the human person's potential to become what he or she is meant to be as fully "selved." Like "Pied Beauty," "As kingfishers catch fire" consists of parallel images from the animate world of birds and insects and the inanimate world of stones and bells. Like "Pied Beauty," it also moves from the particular to the general. The first part of the poem is a long simile. The kingfisher and dragonfly's iridescent radiance, and the reverberating sound of stones dropped into wells and bells chiming to their own particular pitch stand for the involvement of every "mortal thing" in "selving," that is, in expressing its authentic being or its "inscape."

Nature's selving is effortless and spontaneous, it "deals out that being indoors each one dwells," for inner and outer are in perfect harmony. Bird, insect, stone, and bell cannot lie about themselves; there are no hypocritical sparrows! Furthermore, each of these radiates with the fire and reverberates with the sound they have caught from the source of all creation. The "charge" of God that fills the whole world is their legacy, and they cannot help but declare it. Their actions are literally *consonant*; they ring true and resonate with their true selves and the life force itself—their doing *is* their being.

For prayerful pondering

Crying Whát I do is me: for that I came.

This line bids us ask, Can *I* join creation's chorus of, "What I do is me: for that I came," or is there a disparity between what I do and who I am? Am I doing what I have been made to do, and is my doing consonant with my being? What is there within me that I have not yet expressed because of fear? Where is my unlived life? Merely to repeat this line in the manner of *lectio divina* is to affirm and strengthen my destiny as a child of God. In the last line of the octave (the first eight lines), there is an echo of Christ's "I have come that they may have life and have it more abundantly" (Jn 10:10), and this more abundant life is heard through the whole preceding stanza. St. Athanasius wrote that, "The glory of God is a human being fully alive." How do I participate in this fullness of life? What obstacles—unresolved issues, habits, attitudes—hold me back from experiencing that fullness?

This line also prepares us for the sestet (the six-line stanza) that follows. As Christ's abundant life is the *source* of the just one's grace and justice, so the fire of creation is the source of the kingfisher's radiance. *Only* human beings radiate *Christ's* justice, for Christ is their source.

Í say móre: the just man justices;

The person who is receptive to grace is like the kingfisher and dragonfly whose receptivity to fire makes them what they are. The poem goes one better, "say[s] more," because the human being can actually do more than the natural world silently "selving" itself. The human being "Acts...Chríst," with an accent mark to deliberately emphasize this surprising leap. Only the human person who acts with the grace of Christ is able to say with the rest of creation: "What I do is me: for that I came." When I am *just,* true to myself, I am the person God has intended, the most Christlike I can be, for then I am a person who "justices"; *just* is what I am meant to be. I have become justice and thereby *do* justice. When I attend to my true nature (Christ), I act as effortlessly as a dragonfly in fulfilling justice through my actions.

Hopkins' family motto, *Esse quam videri*, "To be rather than to seem," is reflected in this poem where *being* one's true self with the grace of God is *acting* Christ. With grace, my human "acts" are no mere performance, but the reflection of the true being God has always destined me to be—Christ. In his notes from December 1881, Hopkins wrote: "Grace is any action, activity, on God's part by which, in creating or after creating, he carries the creature to or towards the end of its being."[8] If my true identity is hidden "in God's eye," where it is mirrored as Christ, do I seek it in that mirror? Hopkins challenges us to be our true self, to let our true face shine forth—to *be* ourselves rather than merely seem to be.

Not only is this poem about the individual, but its prayerful affirmation extends to the human community reaching toward God. The singular "just man" at the beginning of the sestet turns into many at the end:

> **—for Christ plays in ten thousand places,**
> **Lovely in limbs, and lovely in eyes not his**
> **To the Father through the features of men's**
> **faces.**

The "play" of Christ, Hopkins wrote in spiritual notes of 1881, "is no play but truth. That is Christ *being me* and me being Christ."[9] *Christ's* play creates beauty of body and soul ("lovely in limbs, and lovely in eyes"), so that these ten thousand just persons are as congruent as the dragonflies and swung bells. Their inner congruence is matched by their similarity with each other, creating the dance of all human nature. Christ's play among human-ity is like the swaying of ten thousand trees in harmony with each other and with the wind. Moreover ("Í say more"), they resemble Christ in his Incarnation where the human and divine natures are perfectly united. To-gether they are Christ's Mystical Body, the communion of saints. These lines challenge us to see Christ at play in the eyes, the faces, and the limbs of our brothers and sis-ters. How do I see Christ playing in those I do not find "lovely" or loveable? Dorothy Day continually reminded her collaborators in the Catholic Worker movement to do this by referring to Matthew 25:31–46, "Lord, when did we see you hungry and feed you, or thirsty and give you drink? ...In truth, I tell you as long as you did it to one of the least of these you did it to me."[10]

Christ is the end or goal of creation in its return to its ultimate source, the Father. The ongoing "procession" of Christ into creation and into just human beings is reversed in the poem's final line by the "return" "To the Father."

Hopkins expressed these two movements of Christ in an explanation of the feast of Corpus Christi to Bridges:

> Christ went forth from the bosom of the Father as the Lamb of God and Eucharistic victim to die upon the altar of the cross for the world's ransom; then rising returned leading the procession of the flock redeemed.

The centrality of Christ is most evident in "The Windhover," the poem Hopkins considered "the best thing I ever wrote."[11] He dedicated this poem "To Christ our Lord," and I feel this dedication is key to the poem's significance.

The Windhover

I caught this morning morning's minion, kingdom
 of daylight's dauphin, dapple-dawn-
  drawn Falcon, in his riding
 Of the rolling level underneath him steady
  air, and striding
High there, how he rung upon the rein of a
 wimpling wing
In his ecstasy! then off, off forth on swing,
 As a skate's heel sweeps smooth on a bow-
  bend: the hurl and gliding

Rebuffed the big wind.   My heart in hiding
Stirred for a bird, —the achieve of, the mastery
   of the thing!

Brute beauty and valour and act, oh, air, pride,
      plume, here
   Buckle! AND the fire that breaks from thee
      then, a billion
Times told lovelier, more dangerous, O my
   chevalier!

   No wonder of it: shéer plód makes
      plough down sillion
Shine, and blue-bleak embers, ah my dear,
      Fall, gall themselves, and gash gold-vermilion.

Although this poem presents some of the greatest lin-
guistic difficulties in Hopkins' repertoire, it really amounts
to one sustained vision followed by a series of medita-
tions on that vision. It is, in effect, a *lectio divina* of one,
great scene in nature. Even without deciphering the
meaning of each detail, we can see the kestrel gliding
effortlessly against the dappled dawn sky. We can further
appreciate how noble this creature appears to the poet:
he is the king's falcon, the royal bird, and daylight's prince

"Majestic—as a stallion stalwart"

("dauphin"). Hopkins deliberately uses chivalric language to convey the bird's nobility and power.

Yet, however beautiful the windhover or kestrel may be in flight, Christ's beauty is infinitely surpassing. The capital "AND" of this tercet (three-line stanza) connects the awesome bird to Christ's awful majesty, while at the same time conceals Hopkins' implicit "and yet" which says Christ's "beauty and valour and act" exceed in every way the earthly ("brute beauty") of the bird, and its nobility can never compare to Christ's. Moreover, the fire of the kestrel, as of the kingfisher or dragonfly, literally cannot hold a candle to Christ's, because his fire is not only more beautiful, but also more dangerous. No wonder, says the poet, for every day "plod[ding]" makes the earth's silt shine, and the seemingly extinguished or even dead embers can break into flame again. The poem ends with an image of transformation from burnt-out embers to glowing gold-red fire. Clearly, Hopkins had Christ's radiance in mind when he wrote the last lines of the poem. He expressed this in a sermon, "Poor was his station, laborious his life, bitter his ending: through poverty, through labour, through crucifixion his majesty of nature more shines."[12] So why not see the potential that is Christ's fire, seemingly put out in the crucifixion, gash open to reveal the gold of the Resurrection? Because it is the fire of the Holy Spirit, Christ's fire is not extinguished, even when it plunges into ashes.

For prayerful pondering

When we pray this poem, we enter into a crescendo of word-chimes building up to the climax of the bird's ascent and descent. Then we exceed even that as the bird is ultimately displaced by Christ's attraction and power in our lives. How is Christ the fire of my life? In what ways do I focus on that fire, even when it seems burnt-out? How do I make Christ the luminosity of my work, even when it seems merely "plodding"?

Hopkins' poem, "Hurrahing in Harvest," also centers on his belief that Christ is the summit of creation:

> And the azurous hung hills are his world-
> wielding shoulder
> Majestic—as a stallion stalwart, very-violet-
> sweet!—
> These things, these things were here and but
> the beholder
> Wanting; which two when they once meet,
> The heart rears wings bold and bolder
> And hurls for him, O half hurls earth for him
> off under his feet.

Here, one almost senses Christ's physical presence in nature with the power of a stallion and the sweetness of violets, images that speak of the majesty and mercy of God, which marked Hopkins' life. The poem makes a deliberate bid for the "beholder" to see Christ and to be so moved by him as to become like the windhover spreading its wings effortlessly in the "big wind," or like the stallion that kicks up earth in an ecstatic joy. How often do I *see*, beholding in contemplation, the miracles of God's creation that surround me all the time? In what ways am I the beholder who is "Wanting," either absent or too caught up in my own desires to see?

Handsome Hearts

There is a smaller group of poems under the heading of "Handsome Hearts," a name taken from the title of a poem written by Hopkins' on his return to Oxford as a priest. In this group are poems that celebrate the human person's beauty of body and spirit and a continuation of the theme in "As kingfishers catch fire": Christ "plays in ten thousand places, / Lovely in limbs, and lovely in eyes not his." Hopkins especially appreciated the physical beauty of the body when it was joined with beauty of mind and soul. He once told Bridges:

I think then no one can admire beauty of the body more than I do, and it is of course a comfort to find beauty in a friend or a friend in beauty. But this kind of beauty is dangerous. Then comes the beauty of the mind, such as genius, and this is greater than the beauty of the body and not to call dangerous. And more beautiful than the beauty of the mind is beauty of character, the "handsome heart." The soul may have no other beauty than that which it expresses in the symmetry of the body.[13]

Here again, Hopkins' expresses his belief that the soul expresses its inward beauty in the body, manifesting a sacramental view of the human and natural worlds. In several poems, such as "The Handsome Heart," "Brothers," "Tom Garland," "Harry Ploughman," and "Felix Randal," Hopkins expresses his admiration for the physical beauty of the human body that incarnates the hidden beauty of the human spirit. These poems were written at a time when Hopkins had no access to or time for the beauties of nature, either because he lived in industrial cities or was too involved in parish work. It was in such places and at such times that he found inspiration in the human person. These poems tell us as much about Hopkins the man and priest as they do about the people he chose as the subjects of his poetry. The most success-ful of these poems (in my personal view) is "Felix Randal."

Felix Randal

Felix Randal the farrier, O he is dead then? my
    duty all ended,
Who have watched his mould of man, big-
    boned and hardy-handsome
Pining, pining, till time when reason rambled in
    it and some
Fatal four disorders, fleshed there, all contended?

Sickness broke him.   Impatient he cursed at
    first, but mended
Being anointed and all; though a heavenlier
    heart began some
Months earlier, since I had our sweet reprieve
    and ransom
Tendered to him.   Ah well, God rest him all
    road ever he offended!

This seeing the sick endears them to us, us too
    it endears.

My tongue had taught thee comfort, touch had
   quenched thy tears,
Thy tears that touched my heart, child, Felix,
   poor Felix Randal;

How far from then forethought of, all thy more
   boisterous years,
When thou at the random grim forge, powerful
   amidst peers,
Didst fettle for the great grey drayhorse his
   bright and battering sandal!

In the poem, Hopkins develops a straightforward relationship between a dying man and a priest. The once
"hardy-handsome" blacksmith or "farrier" whose body is
now broken by several diseases is visited by the priest,
the poem's speaker, who brings the last sacraments, "our
sweet reprieve and ransom." Alfred Thomas, S.J., has
compared Hopkins' poetic description of the blacksmith
to the verse in the *Book of Ecclesiasticus:* "The smith at
his anvil is absorbed in his handiwork. The breath of the
fire melts his flesh, and he wastes away in the heat of the
furnace. He batters his ear with the din of the hammer"
(38:28). Hopkins clearly felt that work, honestly and dili-

gently performed, gives God glory. In his notes on the First Principle of the *Exercises* he wrote,

> Smiting on an anvil, sawing a beam, whitewashing a wall, driving horses, sweeping, scouring, everything gives God some glory if being in his grace you do it as your duty.... To lift up the hands in prayer gives God glory, but a man with a dungfork in his hand, a woman with a sloppail, give him glory too. He is so great that all things give him glory if you mean they should.[14]

There is a hint of the developing image of "Pied Beauty" in which Hopkins says "all trádes" give glory to God.

In "Felix Randal," the speaker observes the transformation of an angry man cursing his illness to one whose "heavenlier heart" begins with the "tendering" of the sacraments. "Tendering" conveys both the offering of a gift, the gentleness with which it is offered, and is a play on the metaphor, "ransom"—buying back the sick man.

In the third stanza, we learn the effect this relationship—between the dying man and the priest—had on the priest and the poet. Hopkins has also been moved, "touched," through this channel of communication and comfort for this "child" of God.

Paradoxically, as we approach the actual death of Felix in the last stanza, there is a sudden shift back to the peak of his vitality in "all thy more boisterous years,"

> **How far from then forethought of, all thy**
> **more boisterous years,**
> **When thou at the random grim forge, powerful**
> **amidst peers,**
> **Didst fettle for the great grey drayhorse his**
> **bright and battering sandal!**

How little Felix thought of death when he felt so healthy and powerful, yet his mortality was as much a reality then. Now at the end of his life, memories of his lifetime surface, as past and present mysteriously flow into each other. At the moment of death, we are left with the image of *life* in all its intensity. The poem surges toward this finale, painting an almost unforgettable picture of Felix in his prime, standing at his forge to prepare ("fettle") a shiny horseshoe for *the* "great grey drayhorse." This image is suggestive of the stallion in "Hurrahing in Harvest" whose power is great enough to carry the farrier beyond this world to his reward. The blacksmith who randomly prepared horseshoes now prepares his way to heaven.

For prayerful pondering

In order to pray with this poem, we must become Felix Randal in some way. Although we instinctively shut out the thought of our own death, we now have to envision ourselves on our deathbed or at the moment of death. Nothing awakens us more powerfully to the mystery of being alive than the thought of death. In fact, medieval monks often kept a skull in their cells as a constant reminder of their own death. "Felix Randal" presents the image of a man who comes to terms with his death despite his former vitality and vigor. The poem offers us an invitation to do the same, but now and not on our deathbed. Hopkins, commenting on St. Ignatius' "Principle and Foundation" in the *Spiritual Exercises*, puts it this way:

> This is a comforting thought: we need not wait in fear till death; any day, any minute we bless God for our being or for anything, for food, for sunlight, we do and are what we were meant for, made for—things that give and mean to give God glory. This is a thing to live for. Then make haste so to live.[15]

A prayerful reading of the poem inspires a sense of urgency with regard to our lives, to the present moment as the only one there is. It asks us to "make haste so to live" that we give God glory *now*, that we may awaken to the immense significance of being *alive*. How am I facing my own inevitable death? How am I reconciled to the idea, or how does it haunt me? In what ways am I truly living? How am I striving to acquire Felix's "heavenlier heart," one that is "happy," in life and in death?

Time's Eunuch

Hopkins' last group of poems date from the period of 1885–1889, when he was living in Ireland and struggling with the ravages of deep emotional and physical distress. His spiritual notes from this period testify to his "helpless loathing."[16] These sonnets were dubbed the "terrible sonnets" by Canon Dixon, because he said they were like a "terrible crystal."[17] In reading and praying with these poems of desolation, it is important to acknowledge the depths of despair Hopkins had reached. Hopkins' brutal honesty in facing himself makes these poems so powerful and prayerful. Like the Psalms, they sound the bottommost regions of the human spirit's capacity to endure terrible pain and anguish. Also like the *Psalms* and the *Book of Job*, these poems are prayers addressed to the only One who can hear and heal pain. If the poems Hopkins wrote in Wales came from the heights of exuberance and ecstasy, those written in Dublin came "out of the depths."

During Hopkins' first two years in Ireland he wrote, "Spelt from Sybil's Leaves," a poem with an opaque reference to the *Dies Irae*, the Day of Judgment. In it, earth's "dápple is at énd"; that very dappledness for which the poet had given God glory in "Pied Beauty" is now gone. All the particular beauties, which make up the rich variety of created things have been swept into an overwhelming darkness, perhaps his own dark night of the soul. Hopkins, having wrestled with the worst of his own black despair, realizes that he is wrestling with God. "Carrion Comfort," addresses God with a Job-like quality:

(Carrion Comfort)

Not, I'll not, carrion comfort,
    Despair, not feast on thee;
Not untwist—slack they may be—these last
    strands of man
In me ór, most weary, cry *I can no more.*   I can;
Can something, hope, wish day come, not
    choose not to be.
But ah, but O thou terrible, why wouldst thou
    rude on me
Thy wring-world right foot rock? lay lionlimb
    against me?   scan

With darksome devouring eyes my bruisèd
    bones? and fan,
O in turns of tempest, me heaped there; me
    frantic to avoid thee and flee?

Why?   That my chaff might fly; my grain lie,
    sheer and clear.
Nay in all that toil, that coil, since (seems) I
    kissed the rod,
Hand rather, my heart lo!   lapped strength,
    stole joy, would laugh, chéer.
Cheer whom though?   the hero whose heaven-
    handling flung me, fóot tród
Me? or me that fought him? O which one? is
    it each one?   That night, that year
Of now done darkness I wretch lay wrestling
    with (my God!) my God.

Here, the poet emphatically rejects despair, the food
of the dead, which is only "carrion comfort." The play on
the homophone, "Not" as "knot" at the beginning of the
poem indicates both the speaker's condition, being tied
in knots, and the "last strands" of the fragile knot that
ties him to life and self-hood. Hopkins will not slacken
or cry, *"I can no more,"* which is an ironic reversal of his

earlier "What I do is me, for that I came" in the "King-fishers" poem. His "I can" is a weak, but still positive assertion of the will to live and by the end of the stanza (with the doubling of the "not") there is a firmer resolve.

Then in the second stanza, just when the speaker begins to gather the little remaining strength he has, he sees one he addresses simply as "O thou terrible," the one who rocks the speaker with the same foot that upsets worlds, who lies in wait like a lion with "darksome devouring eyes," and who catches him in the winds of the tempest. Like Job, Hopkins sits on the dung heap, "frantic to avoid" this God of the whirlwind; like Job, he has experienced the loss of everything he holds dear. As with Job, there is an awareness that the struggle is with God.

As the final stanza begins, Hopkins finds an answer to the relentless question of why he is suffering. He remembers a time of great joy in his relationship with God, when he "lapped strength," drank it up as if from God's own hand. All his suffering has been a winnowing of the "chaff" from the "grain"—a purification. On the feast of the Epiphany, January 6, 1889, Hopkins wrote:

> [Christ] baptises with breath and fire, as wheat is winnowed in the wind and sun, and uses...a fan that thoroughly and forever parts the wheat from the

"Mine, O thou lord of life, send my roots rain."

chaff. The grain is either scooped into this or thrown in by another, then tossed out against the wind...the grain lies heaped on one side, the chaff blows away the other, between them the winnower stands.[18]

Although Hopkins begins like Job, huddled helplessly on a heap, by the end of the sonnet he is more like Jacob, entering into mortal combat with the One he now realizes, with mingled awe and horror, is "(my God!) my God." These final words echo Jesus' words on the cross: "My God, my God why hast thou forsaken me?" (Mt 27:46). The speaker has not only come to identify himself with Job in his suffering, and Jacob in his wrestling match, but finally with Christ himself. Who indeed has been cheered by all the joy God brought to him: "The hero...Or me that fought him: O which one? Is it each one?" In his struggle with God, he has come so close to God that he is no longer able to hold himself apart. Like Jacob, Hopkins' mortal battle with the Divine has left him maimed, but renewed. Most importantly, it has enabled him to identify with Christ on the cross. Christ's God-forsakenness is not the meaningless "Despair" of the beginning of the poem, but the opening to Christ's further and here unstated surrender: "Into your hands I commend my spirit" (Lk 23:46).

For prayerful pondering

There are times in every human life when—if we are both truly prayerful and candid with ourselves and with God—a kind of wrestling match is the only appropriate way to remain faithful to God. Like Hopkins and Job, we may feel that God has let us down; he has taken away the very things we find life-sustaining and have prayed so earnestly to keep. When have I been willing to wrestle with God? What honest, probing questions, or doubts, or personal pain have I brought into my relationship with God in prayer? The poem "Carrion Comfort" dares us to reach into the depths of despair, to enter the place where our inner battle is waged and we wonder if life is worth living. In my moments of deepest anguish and suffering, when I may have been tempted to give in to hopelessness, how has God made his presence known? Hopkins shows us the way to open such moments and feelings to God's healing grace.

Rule 8 of St. Ignatius' "Rules on the Discernment of Spirits" states:

> Let him who is in desolation strive to remain in patience, which is the virtue contrary to the troubles which harass him; and let him think that he will shortly be consoled, making diligent efforts against the desolation.[19]

Toward the end of the same year in which he wrote "Carrion Comfort," Hopkins wrote another poem, "My own heart let me more have pity on," that shows how he is trying to be more tender and compassionate with himself:

> My own heart let me more have pity on;   let
> Me live to my sad self hereafter kind,
> Charitable;   not live this tormented mind
> With this tormented mind tormenting yet.

This stanza is remarkable not only for its repetition of the word, "let," which calls attention to the contemplative's "letting be," but also for the triple repetition of the word "torment" in the last lines. It almost seems that the letting up and letting be is ineffective because of the assault of inner torment. But by the end of the poem, the poet has begun to counsel himself:

> let joy size
> At God knows when to God knows what;
>   whose smile
> 's not wrung, see you;   unforeseen times
>   rather—as skies
> Between pie mountains—lights a lovely mile.

The poet here wants to "let joy size," that is, increase. The repeated phrase, "God knows," conveys both his uncertainty about the fulfillment of God's promise and his confidence that God will come through somehow. Hopkins wrote in his notes on St. Ignatius' rules: "Even natural 'consolation' or good spirits come and go without any discoverable reason and certainly, God *could* make us most happy without our knowing what we were happy about."[20] We can never know when God's smile will appear between the mountains "pied" with light and shade, even while we walk in the valley of the shadow of death. God's smile is "not wrung," not extorted from him, but freely given and discovered. In his commentary on Hopkins' poetry, Paul Mariani writes: "The wedge of light between the mountains also suggests God's enormous smile, which, when it comes, is completely disproportionate to what was reasonable expected."[21] In times of depression, we may need to learn to be kind to ourselves, to develop an expectancy about small joys that may unexpectedly come to light up our days, and to let those joys "size," grow greater day by day.

Where "Carrion Comfort" hints at Hopkins' past relationship with God, Poem 74 ("Thou art indeed just, Lord"), forms a prayer that addresses God directly. The poem begins with the heartfelt prayer of the Prophet Jeremiah, which is translated in the first two lines:

Justus quidem tu es, Domine, si disputem
tecum; verumtamen justa loquar ad te: Quare
via impiorum prosperatur? &c.

Thou art indeed just, Lord, if I contend
With thee; but, sir, so what I plead is just.
Why do sinners' ways prosper? and why must
Disappointment all I endeavor end?

Wert thou my enemy, O thou my friend,
How wouldst thou worse, I wonder, than thou dost
Defeat, thwart me?   Oh, the sots and thralls of
    lust
Do in spare hours more thrive than I that spend,
Sir, life upon thy cause.   See, banks and brakes
Now, leavèd how thick! lacèd they are again
With fretty chervil, look, and fresh wind shakes
Them; birds build—but not I build; no, but
    strain,
Time's eunuch, and not breed one work that
    wakes,
Mine, O thou lord of life, send my roots rain.

The intense battle of "Carrion Comfort" is over, and
a milder questioning ensues. In Jeremiah 12:1, the prophet

prays toward the end of his life, which has been dedicated to God and seems to have yielded only rejection and futility while evil people have thrived. Hopkins' poem expresses a similar feeling of betrayal. Written in March 1889, following his retreat and two months before his final illness, Hopkins, like Jeremiah, begins an almost legal argument with God, addressing the Lord as "sir." He has spent and has certainly been spent, giving his whole life to the cause of God, but he feels no corresponding fulfillment. The question in the second stanza: "Wert thou my enemy, O thou my friend," recalls St. Teresa of Avila's equally daring declaration in a moment of discouragement: "It is no wonder you have so few friends, my God, since this is how you treat them."

In this "terrible sonnet," more than the other, Hopkins turns to nature for images to compare with his own life: riverbanks, thick with cow parsley and other growth, stir with the wind. Here we cannot help but hear an echo of Psalm 1:

> Happy are those who do not follow the advice of
>   the wicked...
> but their delight is in the law of the LORD,
> and on his law they meditate day and night.
> They are like trees planted by streams of water,

which yield their fruit in due season,
and their leaves do not wither (1:2–3).

The next image of birds that take some of the lacy leaves shaken by the wind to build their nests, contrasts with the poet's inability to be moved by this "fresh wind" or to build anything lasting: "birds build, but not I build." Perhaps the "not" precedes the subject to negate any actual achievement—"not/naught is what I build."

The arresting phrase, "Time's eunuch," can be found in a letter Hopkins wrote to Bridges in 1885: "If I could but get on, if I could but produce work I should not mind its being buried, silenced, and going no further; but it kills me to be time's eunuch and never to beget."[22] On retreat in 1889, Hopkins entered these words of utter despair and melancholy into his personal retreat notes:

> I could therefore do no more than repeat *Justus es,
> Domine, et rectum judicium tuum* and the like.... All
> my undertakings miscarry: I am like a straining eu-
> nuch.... O my God, look down on me.[23]

The last line of the poem contains its most forceful and poignant prayer: "Mine, O thou lord of life, send my roots rain." Again, in a letter to Bridges, Hopkins wrote, "There is a point with me in matters of any size when I must absolutely have encouragement as much as crops rain."[24] "Mine" at the beginning of the line addresses itself both to the Lord who has always been his and to the poet's parched, dried-up roots, indicating his intimate relationship with God, despite his aridity. It certainly speaks of Hopkins' moving and unfailing loyalty to his Lord throughout his whole life, even in the heart of his darkness. Standing at the beginning of the line, "Mine" calls attention to the fact that this mysterious union has survived Hopkins' last terrible trial. At the end of his life, Hopkins could have said with St. Paul: "For I am certain of this: neither death nor life, nor angels, nor principalities, nothing already in existence and nothing still to come, nor any power, nor the heights nor the depths, nor any created thing whatever, will be able to come between us and the love of God, known to us in Christ Jesus our Lord" (Rom 8:38–39). The tragic irony of Hopkins' life is that, in retrospect, he bred not one but many "work[s] that wake," which have the power to wake us.

For prayerful pondering

This poem is studded with questions that can be directly applied to our own life of prayer. Those who have dedicated their lives to God and not always felt the consideration of a human reward might well want to ask,

"Why do sinners' ways prosper?" or "why must / Disappointment all I endeavor end?" These real questions, posed "out of the depths," echo questions raised by the psalmists and prophets, though they might seem irreverent to some. And yet, in all the disappointments, the lack of tangible rewards, and the sterility of his efforts, Hopkins trusted and turned to God, who alone was his hope. Can I name the obstacles in my life that prevent me from believing in the love of God? In the presence of personal disappointment or the seeming futility of my efforts, what can I do to keep myself focused on God's love? If I feel I've done so much for God and yet see others "prosper," people I consider less worthy of God's blessing, can I name God's blessings in my life?

Conclusion

It is my hope that these reflections on the poetry of Gerard Manley Hopkins will enable you to return to them in a more prayerful engagement with them. Perhaps this book will have encouraged you to turn to other poems in this poet's rich and powerful collection, to find ever new ways in which they can help you to pray with them and through them. They are a challenge to those who read and pray them, in this twenty-first century, to celebrate the "dappled things" of the world, to see Christ at play in nature and in the faces of others, to appreciate the goodness of the "handsome hearts" among us, and to grieve before God the real pains of human existence. In their exceptional ability to move us to prayer, Hopkins' poems are vehicles and sacraments of grace.

CHAPTER 5

Steps for Reading Poetry in a Holy Way

1. Hopkins advised those who read poetry, to do so "slowly, strongly, marking the rhythms and fetching out the syllables." The first task in approaching a poem as prayer, then, is to say it aloud and to *really* hear it. Hear the play of sounds and rhymes and rhythms. Are its rhythms anxious and hurried or careful and slow? Where does the poem want the reader to pause, or to move toward a climactic word? Let the poem's rhythm remind you of the rhythm of your heartbeat. This humble, material level of the poem is a crucial part of its meaning.

2. Slow down. Read with the care and full attention of *"lectio divina."* Use the mind's "abiding energy" to stay with the images and sounds, letting them penetrate your conscious and unconscious mind at ever deeper levels. Poetry is not a linear but cyclical reading. Go over the poem again and again, "letting lines and stanzas be left in the memory and superficial impressions deepened" as Hopkins has suggested. Take one line or image of the poem and say it repeatedly, as a kind of mantra or refrain, offering it to God from your heart in prayer.

3. Look for the "inscape" of a poem in its form. Look at its shape on the page, its long or short lines. Begin to connect the form with the content. See how the meaning is incarnated in the form, sounds, and images. Pay attention even to the connectors of the verse—the simple "ands," "buts," and "yets." Are they creating contrast and antithesis or resemblance and relationships? Is the poem enacting a unity or disunity and brokenness?

4. Read with a readiness to be surprised, "instressed" as Hopkins put it. Hopkins wanted his poems to be full of surprises, and this humbling response to poetry disarms us of our pretensions to knowledge. Experience the feelings of a poem, its ecstasy or earnestness or playfulness. Let them open your heart.

5. Play with the images. Try an "image explosion" and write down your own associations with an image until the meaning is expanded and deepened for you. Remember that the poem is offering itself now to *your* interpretation, and no one meaning, not even the author's, exhausts it. Take one image from the poem and let it lead you into silence or into the spontaneous arising of your own images in prayer.

6. Create a ritual around the reading and praying of poetry: lighting a candle, clearing a space on a desk, sanctifying a small period of time for this purpose, reading a poem aloud to one other person so that, together, you enter into the silence around the poem.

7. Pray a poem in response to the news. Offer the poem as a silent gesture of sanity in a sometimes not so sane world.

Suggested Poems for Praying

Angelou, Maya

Thank You, Lord

Berry, Wendell

Meditation in the Spring Rain
A Purification

Dickinson, Emily

I taste a liquor never brewed—
I never saw a moor
The Chariot
The daisy follows soft the sun (XXXIV)
Wild Nights—Wild Nights!

Dillard, Annie

Teaching a Stone to Talk

Levertov, Denise

Lyon, George Ella

Norris, Kathleen

Rilke, Rainer Maria

> *The Book of Hours: Love Poems to God*
> *Sonnets to Orpheus*

Rumi

> *Say Yes Quickly*

Sachs, Nelly

> *Your Eyes, O my beloved*
> *Someone*
> *Rushing at times like flames*
> *But perhaps God needs the longing*

Tsvetaeva, Marina

> *God (3)*

Vaughn, Henry

> *The Night*

Wilbur, Richard

> *Love Calls Us to the Things of This World*

Notes

Chapter 1
Poetry as Prayer

1. From T. S. Eliot's "The Dry Salvages." One line adds, "The hint half guessed, the gift half understood, is Incarnation."

2. Quoted in David Whyte, *The Heart Aroused: Poetry and the Preservation of the Soul in Corporate America* (New York: Currency Doubleday, 1994), 18.

3. Gerard Manley Hopkins, "Parmenides," in *The Journals and Papers of Gerard Manley Hopkins*, ed. Humphry House, Completed by Graham Storey (London: Oxford University Press, 1959), 127 [hereafter *Journals*].

4. In *Little Girls in Church* (Pittsburgh: University of Pittsburgh Press, 1995).

5. Quoted by Kathleen Norris, Gethsemani, September 1999.

6. He was to call this design by his own unique word, their "inscape."

7. "On the Origin of Beauty," in *Journals*, 109.

8. *The Letters of Gerard Manley Hopkins to Robert Bridges*, ed. with intro. by Claude C. Abbott (London: Oxford University Press, 1955), 50 [hereafter *Letters I*].

9. Frank McAloon, S.J., "Prayer, Poetry, and Hopkins," International Hopkins Summer School, Monasterevin, Ireland (July 2000), stated, "those who pray with poetry open themselves to the possibility of transformation."

Chapter 2
Gerard Manley Hopkins: A Life

1. He writes of this to his parents: "Clarke, my co-victim, was flogged, struck off the confirmation, and fined £1; I was deprived of my room for ever, sent to bed at half-past nine till further orders, and ordered to work *only* in the school room, not even in the school library...." quoted in Norman White, *Hopkins: A Literary Biography* (Oxford: Clarendon Press, 1992), 35. White mentions that Hopkins "made a habit of being unpunctual at his duties on Sunday mornings..." (34).

2. Ibid.

3. *The Correspondence of Gerard Manley Hopkins and R. W. Dixon*, ed. Claude C. Abbott (London: Oxford University Press, 1935), 12 [hereafter *Letters II*].

4. *Further Letters of Gerard Manley Hopkins*, ed. Claude C. Abbott, 2nd edition (Oxford: Oxford University Press, 1956), 69 [hereafter *Letters III*].

5. "On the Signs of Health and Decay in the Arts," [an essay written for the Master of Balliol, 1864], in *Journals*, 77.

6. Ibid., 138.

7. Ibid., 146.

8. *Letters III*, 16–17.

9. *Letters I*, 16–17.

10. Ibid., 19.

11. *Journals*, 165.

12. *Letters III*, 231.

13. Ibid., 232.

14. Ibid., 408.

15. *Journals*, Nov. 6, 1865, 71.

16. *Sermons and Devotional Writings of Gerard Manley Hopkins*, ed. Christopher Devlin, S.J. (London: Oxford University Press, 1959), 119 [hereafter *Sermons*].

17. "A Meditation on the Two Standards," *The Spiritual Exercises of St. Ignatius*, 75.

18. "Contemplation for Attaining Love," *Spiritual Exercises*, 104.

19. *Journals*, 258.

20. *Letters II*, 14.

21. *Letters I*, 43.

22. *Journals*, 221.

23. "Introduction," *Sermons*, xiii.

24. *Letters I*, 47.

25. Ibid., 66.

26. *Letters II*, 88.

27. Ibid., 89–90.

28. "A Meditation on Two Standards," *Spiritual Exercises*, 75.

29. In a letter to Canon Dixon, July 1886, he spoke of Christ, "his plans

were baffled, his hopes dashed, and his work was done by being broken off undone" (*Letters II*, 137–8).

30. *Sermons*, 253.

31. White, 362.

32. *Letters I*, 221.

33. *Sermons*, 262.

34. Ibid., 455.

35. *Letters III*, 196–197.

36. Ibid., 253–254.

Chapter 3
Priest and Poet

1. *Journals*, 254.

2. Ibid., 199.

3. *Journals*, 221.

4. *Letters III*, 306.

5. Ibid., 230.

6. *Sermons*, 122–123.

7. *Letters I*, 66.

8. "Notes on the Contemplation for Obtaining Love," *Sermons*, 195.

9. Pierre Teilhard de Chardin, "Christ in the World of Matter," *Hymn of the Universe* (New York and Evanston: Harper and Row), 1965.

10. As he wrote in his spiritual notes of Sept. 5, 1883: "God is good and the stamp, seal, or instress he sets on each scape is of *right, good,* or of *bad, wrong,*" *Sermons*, 139.

11. *Letters I*, 160.

12. *Sermons*, 263.

13. *Letters I* (Oct. 24, 1883), 187–188.

14. *Sermons*, 129.

15. *Letters I*, 156.

16. *Sermons*, 197.

17. *Letters II*, 137–138.

18. Walter J. Ong, S.J. in *Hopkins, the Self, and God* (Toronto: University

of Toronto Press, 1986), treats the subject of *kenosis* as central to Hopkins' concept of the Incarnation and alludes to Hopkins' "elaborate theory about a cosmic Eucharistic presence of Christ." (pp. 112–116 and 119).

19. *Letters I*, 175.

20. *Sermons*, p. 137–8

21. *Letters I*, p. 175.

22. Compare Devlin's remarks that "His poetic genius was his very essence, his 'inscape,' his special likeness to the Divine Essence. Yet Hopkins the Jesuit behaved to Hopkins the poet as a Victorian husband might to a wife of whom he had cause to be ashamed" (*Sermons*, 119).

Chapter 4
Praying with the Sonnets

1. *Letters I*, 90.

2. *Spiritual Exercises*, 82.

3. *Sermons*, 239.

4. Quoted in "Notes" to *The Poems of Gerard Manley Hopkins, Fourth Edition*, ed. W. H. Gardner and N. H. Mackenzie (Oxford: Oxford University Press, 1970), 263.

5. *Journals*, 290.

6. Ibid., 195.

7. *Letters I*, 299.

8. *Sermons*, 152.

9. Ibid., 154.

10. See *Dorothy Day: Selected Writings*, ed. Robert Ellsberg (Maryknoll, NY: Orbis Books, 1993).

11. Quoted in "Notes" to *The Poems, Fourth Edition*, 266.

12. *Sermons*, 37.

13. *Letters I*, 95.

14. *Sermons*, 240–241.

15. Ibid.

16. *Sermons*, 263.

17. *Letters II*, 80.

18. Ibid., 268.

19. *Spiritual Exercises*, 130.

20. Ibid., 204 and 207.

21. *A Commentary on the Complete Poems of Gerard Manley Hopkins* (Ithaca, NY: Cornell University Press, 1970), 240.

22. *Letters I*, 221–222.

23. *Sermons*, 262.

24. *Letters I*, 218–219.

Maria Lichtmann received her Ph.D. in religious studies from Yale University, doing her dissertation on the spirituality and poetics of Gerard Manley Hopkins. She writes and teaches at Appalachian State University in Boone, NC. She is the author of *The Contemplative Poetry of Gerard Manley Hopkins* (Princeton, 1989), as well as numerous articles on the mystics. She is married to Robert Schneider and has two wonderful grandsons.

THE POETRY AS PRAYER SERIES

offers poetic verse as a means to prayer
exploring the connection
between culture and religion,
creativity and mysticism, literature and life.

Included in the series:

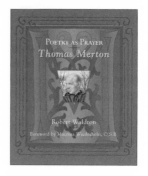

Poetry as Prayer
The Psalms
By Basil Pennington, OCSO
Artwork by Helen Kita
#5927-3
paperback, 160 pages

Poetry as Prayer
Thomas Merton
By Robert Waldron
Artwork by Helen Kita
#5919-2
paperback, 200 pages

Each volume in the series offers a particular poet's writings as a means to deepen one's prayer, since poetry—like prayer—is a "language of the heart."

Features:
- *Insightful spiritual guide*
- *Passages introduce the reader to a unique experience of prayer*

Price: $9.95 each ($16.25 Canada)

Poetry as Prayer
Jessica Powers
By Bishop Robert F. Morneau
Artwork by Joseph Karlik
#5921-4
paperback, 176 pages

Poetry as Prayer
The Hound of Heaven
By Robert Waldron
Artwork by Anthony Lobosco
#5914-1
paperback, 160 pages

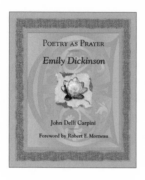

Poetry as Prayer
Emily Dickinson
By John Delli Carpini
Artwork by Armanda Santos, FSP
#5935-4
paperback, 160 pages

Poetry as Prayer
Gerard Manley Hopkins
By Maria Lichtmann
Artwork by Douglas Bertanzetti
#5936-2
paperback, 160 pages

...with more titles to follow!

To order, contact:

BOOKS & MEDIA

50 Saint Pauls Avenue, Boston, MA 02130-3491
1-800-876-4463
www.pauline.org

or from the Center nearest you.

auline
BOOKS & MEDIA

The Daughters of St. Paul operate book and media centers at the following addresses. Visit, call or write the one nearest you today, or find us on the World Wide Web, www.pauline.org

CALIFORNIA
3908 Sepulveda Blvd, Culver City, CA
 90230 310-397-8676
5945 Balboa Avenue, San Diego, CA
 92111 858-565-9181
46 Geary Street, San Francisco, CA
 94108 415-781-5180
FLORIDA
145 S.W. 107th Avenue, Miami, FL
 33174 305-559-6715
HAWAII
1143 Bishop Street, Honolulu, HI
 96813 808-521-2731
Neighbor Islands call: 800-259-8463
ILLINOIS
172 North Michigan Avenue,
 Chicago, IL 60601
 312-346-4228
LOUISIANA
4403 Veterans Blvd, Metairie, LA
 70006 504-887-7631
MASSACHUSETTS
885 Providence Hwy,
 Dedham, MA 02026
 781-326-5385
MISSOURI
9804 Watson Road,
 St. Louis, MO 63126
 314-965-3512

NEW JERSEY
561 U.S. Route 1, Wick Plaza,
 Edison, NJ 08817
 732-572-1200
NEW YORK
150 East 52nd Street, New York, NY
 10022 212-754-1110
78 Fort Place, Staten Island, NY
 10301 718-447-5071
PENNSYLVANIA
9171-A Roosevelt Blvd, Philadelphia,
 PA 19114 215-676-9494
SOUTH CAROLINA
243 King Street, Charleston, SC
 29401 843-577-0175
TENNESSEE
4811 Poplar Avenue, Memphis, TN
 38117 901-761-2987
TEXAS
114 Main Plaza, San Antonio, TX
 78205 210-224-8101
VIRGINIA
1025 King Street, Alexandria, VA
 22314 703-549-3806
CANADA
3022 Dufferin Street, Toronto, Ontario,
 Canada M6B 3T5 416-781-9131
1155 Yonge Street, Toronto, Ontario,
 Canada M4T 1W2 416-934-3440

¡También somos su fuente para libros, videos y música en español!